The
SOUTH
FORK

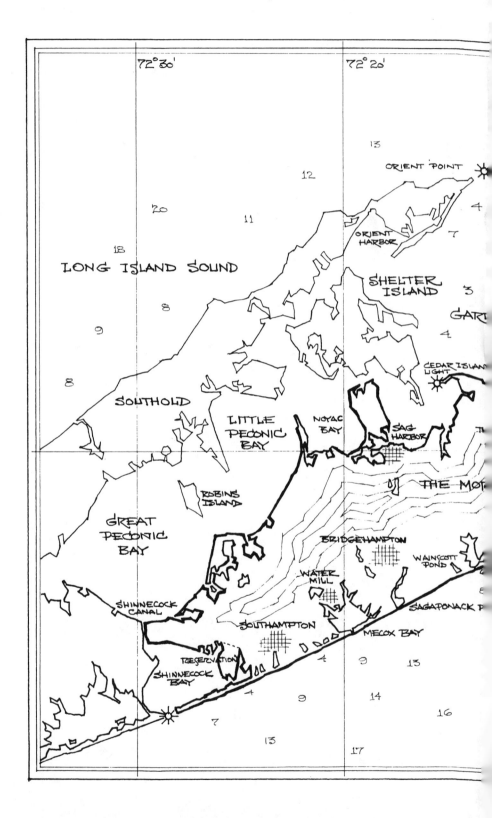

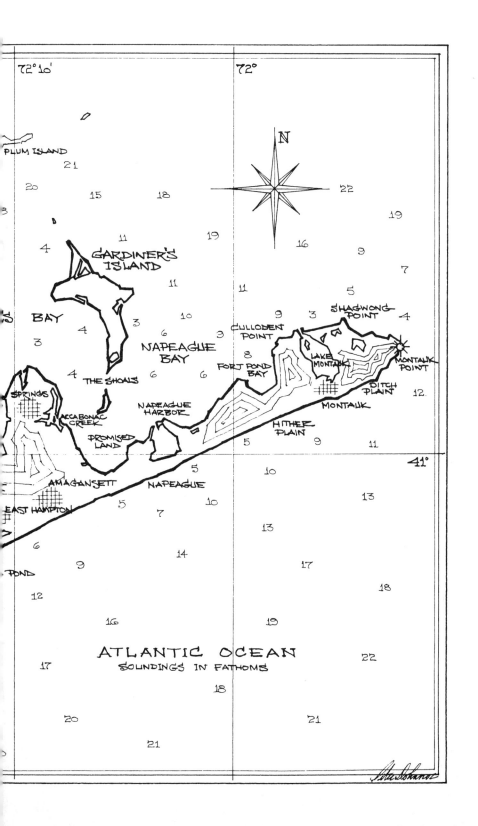

PUBLISHER'S NOTE

This is the first paperback publication of Everett Rattray's classic. *The South Fork* was first published in 1979 and it is a tribute to Mr. Rattray's scholarship that little updating is needed. The reader will note that the population figures cited in the Foreword and on page six have significantly increased in the past decade. Also, as the author hoped (page 109), the banning of DDT has brought back the osprey population. Aside from these details, *The South Fork* stands as an enduring study of the land that Everett Rattray loved.

Everett Tennant Rattray was born at Southampton, Long Island, in 1932, the son of a San Francisco Scott and an East Hampton Edwards. He lived his life in East Hampton, with absences for attendance at Dartmouth College, the Navy, and the Columbia University Graduate School of Journalism. From 1958 until his death in 1980, he was editor and then publisher of the *East Hampton Star*. His wife, Helen, continues as publisher of that distinguished journal. Mr. Rattray was also the author of the novel, *The Adventures of Jeremiah Dimon: A Novel of Old East Hampton*, published in 1985 by Pushcart Press.

Bill Henderson
Pushcart Press

The
SOUTH
FORK

*The Land and the People of
Eastern Long Island*

EVERETT T. RATTRAY
Illustrations by Peter Dohanos

PUSHCART

For
Grandma
who passed down
the storytelling urge

We had great comfort and reliefe from the most honorable of the English nation heare about us; soe that seinge wee yet live, and both of us beinge now oulde, and not that wee at any time have given him any thinge to gratifie his fatherly love, care and charge, we havinge nothing left that is worth his acceptance but a small tract of land . . .

> Deed from Wyandanch, Sachem of the Montauks, to Lion Gardiner, for ten square miles comprising the present Town of Smithtown, Long Island (population 125,000). Dated July 14, 1659.

Foreword

PROBABLY THE WHOLE FASHIONABLE WORLD in America and Europe has heard of the Hamptons, the chic Hamptons. But the term is a gossip columnist's, rarely used by the native, who prefers to describe the place of his or her birth as the South Fork, the southerly of Long Island's split-fin eastern promontories, and who thinks of the different villages as separate and unique.

Two hours by car from Manhattan (except during the summer traffic), the South Fork includes all the Hamptons save West. Behind its tennis courts, between its beach houses, beneath its society veneer is a beautiful part of the world with an unusual past. It is an island of an island, separated by the Shinnecock Canal from the rest of Long Island, a 30-mile strip of hills, dunes, and woods with a year-round population of perhaps 30,000 souls, fiercely proud of a heritage largely neglected in the history textbooks, and quick to bristle at the condescension of the summer visitor.

Americans on holiday are careless of their surroundings, likely to be interested in them only as part of the ambience of a pleasant summer; there are few true sightseers among the Long Island summer-population vacationers. The South Fork has been a resort for a century or more, frequented by the wealthy and well educated of America, yet its extraordinary physical nature usually impresses them merely as a pleasant place with fine beaches; they recognize its lively history only where it is visible—as in a windmill—and ignore its individualistic population. Indeed, the "summer people" are often puzzled and sometimes irritated to discover that the place is actually inhabited in the winter; they like to imagine there was nothing before they came, and will be nothing upon their departure.

Yet the study of our world, as it was and is, is really the study of ourselves, and a good place to begin is on native ground. The South Fork is native now to a relative handful; it could be native to thousands more if they would undertake the necessary naturalization exercises, which include some long looks beneath the surface of things.

E. T. Rattray

The
SOUTH
FORK

Chapter

I

THE LONG ISLAND RAIL ROAD published in 1902 an aerial view of its domain. The Wrights were a year from flight; no man had ever risen to the altitude to which the view pretends, three or four miles above the Atlantic somewhere south of Brooklyn. But the artist, J. W. Falls, correctly anticipated the vista that commercial aviation would make commonplace within a lifetime.

His Long Island—in its printed version a poster a foot high and four feet long—is green with fields and woods, set between an ocean of stippled blue and a paler Sound. At the top of artist Falls's map, mountains, from the Catskills at the left to the White Mountains at the right, loom dark below fleecy cumulus clouds tinged with pink. The artist's clouds, however, would have to be miles taller than the greatest thunderhead to be in proportion, and his Atlantic is dotted with schooners and steamers which, if drawn to scale, would be several miles from stem to stern.

No roads are shown, for this is a railroad's view; Long Island's hamlets, villages and cities, from the Montauk settlement at the right to the city of Brooklyn at the left, are linked only by the various branches of the LIRR, themselves drawn as much out of proportion as are the piers at Coney Island and the Lighthouse at Fire Island Inlet. J. W. Falls's problem was that he was dealing with an island truly long, stretching 118 miles from Bay Ridge in Brooklyn to Montauk Point.

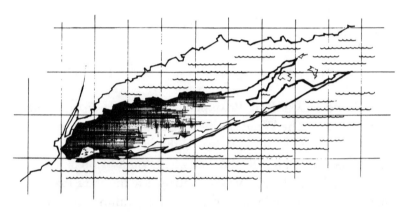

A WHALE NUZZLING MANHATTAN

The Long Island Rail Road view—understandably for an enterprise whose domain then as now centered on the populous western end of its Island—emphasizes that suburban area. This Long Island is a whale with a healthy trunk and skull, its forehead nuzzling Manhattan and its jaws about to bite Staten Island. This whale's flukes, the North and South Forks at the eastern end of Long Island, dangle off in the distance toward

Buzzard's Bay and Cape Cod in Massachusetts, which can be seen dimly at the upper right of the map. They are weak and spindly, trailing like the tail of an aquarium damselfish rather than of a leviathan.

A more distant view of Long Island, on a Mercator's projection of the North Atlantic or from a satellite, shows a minnow, not a whale, but a healthy minnow, its blunt brow pushing against the mainland at the center of the great curve in the East Coast of the United States called the New York Bight. This sturdy creature's tail-fins are healthier than the whale's, kicking a bit higher than its head, for Long Island runs from southwest to northeast. If the minnow is swimming, it is tumbling in its wake Block Island, Martha's Vineyard, and Nantucket.

To its north lies Connecticut, which has no true seacoast, only Sound coast, blocked from the full force of the Atlantic by Long Island. The Island's eastern extremity, Montauk Point, is closer to Boston than it is to Manhattan, and the citizen of Wilmington, Delaware, Wilkes-Barre, Pennsylvania, or Hartford, Connecticut, lives closer to Times Square than the Montauker does. The latter is also a resident of East Hampton Town, the easternmost town on the Island and truly a town, not a township. In East Hampton, even today, three quarters of the newborn are offspring of parents themselves native. And like most of its fellow towns on Long Island, it was established as an independent republic in embryo—an offspring of the Massachusetts Bay Colony—long before there was a United States with a township system, before there was a New York.

East Hampton shares the South Fork with Southampton Town, as Southold shares the North Fork with Riverhead. Between the Forks lies Shelter Island, a town to itself and so named because it was literally a shelter to the Quakers during the New England persecutions at the end of the seventeenth century. The East End Towns of Long Island still dream of the days when they were on their own, looked to New England only for advice, and to Manhattan, Dutch or English for little but trouble.

West of the East End Towns lies massive Brookhaven Town, the outer line of suburbia. There are four other suburban towns in Suffolk County, which occupies the bulk of the Island and is insulated from New York City by Nassau County. Consider the demographics: the western two thirds of Long Island, including Brooklyn and Queens, which are within the New York City limits, Nassau and the five West End Towns of Suffolk, has a population of 7,300,000. The eastern and still rural third, the five East End Towns, has a population of 110,000.

Dr. Arthur Terry of East Hampton, who lengthened his years to eighty-eight by the judicious use of a device of his own invention, a teeterboard that promoted the flow of blood to the brain, was musing on the East End's place in the sun, with his feet higher than his head, one day a decade ago. It suddenly came to him that a cartographic injustice had been done; nowhere in East Hampton was there recognition of the passing of 41 degrees north latitude across the town from east to west. He prevailed upon the highway department, and a cross within a circle, representing the juncture of 41 degrees north latitude and 72 degrees 11 minutes west longitude, was shortly painted upon the paving in the parking lot at Three Mile Harbor, off Gardiner's Bay just beyond East Hampton Village, and appropriately inscribed.

Long Island thus lies about as far above the equator as Madrid, Naples, Peking, and the northern marches of California, and as far west of the prime meridian at Greenwich as Quebec City to the north and Port-au-Prince, Haiti, to the south. The Gulf Stream parallels its coast some fifty miles offshore, alleviating its winters, and its surrounding waters are slow to warm up in the spring, cooling its summers. Long Island lies close enough to the usual track of coastal hurricanes to have been struck by many since records were first kept. It is a place where geography has molded history into odd shapes, and where history has produced odd people, as is to be expected of any backwater.

For backwater is what much of Long Island once was, and its East End still is. Yet in this backwater are preserved memories of a time when it was a fulcrum for several cultures and nations on the new frontier of North America. Long before that time, the Island had been part of a geological frontier, where the great Wisconsin glaciation met the sea. There was no one there to tell the tale, but it can be read today in the hills and the plains of potato fields, where they are not buried by the eastern advance of suburbia, whose extent is marked in clear weather by a bank of smog visible at mid-Island, near the village of Patchogue. Transatlantic pilots coming into Kennedy Airport, which was built near the focal point of the 1902 Long Island Rail Road view, sight the bank of haze from hundreds of miles offshore.

Chapter II

MAN FIRST CAME TO LONG ISLAND before it was an island, filtering in, insinuating himself toward the sea from the west and north, stepping dry-shod across the future channel the Dutch would call Hell Gate and skirting the lake the English would name Long Island Sound. The first coming was soon after the great glacier, 10,000 or 12,000 years ago, at a time when mastodons still roamed the broad pasture sloping toward an Atlantic surging many miles beyond the present beach line, which would diminish and become Long Island. They came from Asia, or at least their ancestors did, but this origin was probably many generations forgotten by the time the continent was crossed.

Man came again to Long Island in late April of the year 1524, when Giovanni da Verrazano's vessel *La Dauphine* sailed out of the great river we give Henry Hudson's name and turned east, following the coast. Verrazano had hugged the beach all the way north from Florida on that voyage; he had gazed across the Outer Banks between Cape Lookout and Cape Hatteras, and mistaken Pamlico Sound for the Pacific. The weather would

have been settled as *La Dauphine* moved east along the Long
Island shore before a southwest breeze off the ocean or heeled to
the northwesters that bright, clear spring days bring to this
corner of North America. Verrazano and his men would have
seen the long ridge of the glacial moraine inland, most likely
topped with tall trees, and the smoke from cook fires ashore.
Late April was corn-planting time in the fields behind the long
ribbon of pale-white beach.

Seeing, they were also seen, these first Europeans. A month
earlier Verrazano, whose coasting habits in dangerous waters
show him to have been a skilled and daring, or perhaps foolish,
mariner, had anchored in an open roadstead off the strip of
southern beach he thought separated the Atlantic from the
Pacific. A boat was sent in to search for fresh water. Prevented
from landing by heavy surf, it lay to outside the breakers while
a sailor swam ashore with "paper, glasses, bells and such trifles"
for the watching natives. The swimmer was caught by a comber
and thrown insensible upon the shore.

The Indians (one supposes Verrazano thought them East
Indians) carried the sailor up on the beach, and prepared a fire;
his shipmates thought he would be cooked. Instead, he was
warmed, embraced, and made ready for his swim back to the boat;
the Indians helped him into the water.

Verrazano apparently did not land on Long Island. Passing
Montauk, he rounded Block Island as the weather deteriorated,
and entered Narragansett Bay, a contemporary chronicle tells us,
with the help of an Indian pilot. A pilot would have to have had
some comprehension of the vessel's draught, its management, its
essence. How does this square with our stories that the Indians
regarded the Europeans and their ships as the fulfillment of a
prophecy, great white birds upon the sea? The natives are said
to have politely ignored, in some places, what was beyond their
ken at first confrontation. But there is a vast difference between

this and helping out a waterlogged French sailor or piloting a 100-ton ship around rock ledges into harbor.

Our conception of the European arrival on these shores, on Long Island and elsewhere, is tidier and more simplistic than the truth may be. The Spanish had conquered Mexico three years before that spring of 1524. As we have come to realize, there was considerable native trade and cultural interchange through the center of North America; the sophisticated civilization of the people we call Moundbuilders, which echoed the cultures of Central and South America, occupied a large part of what it later suited white Americans to refer to as a howling wilderness.

No matter what wonders lay hidden inland, the Europeans— Dutch, English, Spanish, Italian, Viking perhaps—arrived by water, and their hearts must have sunk at the immensity of the new land, green trees against a gray-blue horizon stretching ahead indefinitely. From the beach, the aborigines must have either watched impassively, danced in excitement, shaken in fear, consulted their wise men, or turned their backs in ostentatious scorn; one would like to know which. They were people of the land in a way that it is nearly impossible for us to comprehend. Were there those among them who realized that this was all to change, that their long day was ending?

A long day it had been. Archaeologists working at the Koster site in southern Illinois say that men arrived there some 8,500 years ago, shortly after the departure of the last great glaciers, and lived on the same ground with little interruption until close to modern times. The evidence suggests that their civilization was stable and far more advanced than is commonly supposed. Over 5,000 years ago, for example, the population of this area on the Illinois River lived in the sort of wattle-and-daub houses that were used by most Europeans through the Middle Ages. There is no particular reason to believe that the aboriginal inhabitants we persist in miscalling Indians were any less advanced in the coastal areas.

Until they had their first contact with Europeans—those strange creatures divorced from the land—the native Americans had been separated from the rest of the world's population (except for perhaps a few stray contacts through shipwreck or an occasional deliberate voyage) since long before the building of the Pyramids, for perhaps 10,000, even 20,000 years when Stonehenge was built.

The people of this continent 4,000, 6,000 or 8,000 years ago appear to have lived a life roughly comparable in its mixture of technology and superstition to that of their European and Asian counterparts. The Americans, however, were spared the great migrations and strife that swept across the Eurasian landmass, the stress and conflict that force-fed the development of new tools and new ideas. Their world changed slowly over the centuries, and their lack of resistance to the diseases of Europe was matched by the fragility of their social institutions, which could survive only in isolation. A few Spanish horsemen toppled empires in Central and South America; in North America the mere approach of Europeans sufficed, and the civilization found by De Soto along the Mississippi in 1541 was in tatters long before the seaboard colonists pushed west in search of new farm-land two centuries later.

At the time Europeans settled on the Eastern Seaboard, the Indians were probably as knowledgeable about the whites as the whites were about the reds, and perhaps more so, but it was knowledge that had been acquired overnight in terms of the Indians' long occupation of the land. The Indian learned quickly; he had a quite unchristian interest in human behavior, an extension of his necessary obsession, as a hunter, with animal behavior. And just as Indian legends were full of the antics and wiles of wolves, bears, and other quarry, so the red man came to be amused by the white, an adversary more dangerous than any bear—a sense of humor more often found in empire losers than in empire winners.

The early Europeans in North America were constantly surprised by evidence of previous intercourse between the races. The Pilgrims were welcomed to Plymouth by Samoset, speaking broken English. He introduced them to Squanto, who spoke better English; he had indeed been kidnapped and sent to Spain as a slave, was freed by friars, and had then visited England before returning to North America. All up and down the coast it was the same: a corpse dressed in European clothes found in a shallow grave on Cape Cod . . . a broken dagger with an Italian grip in Maine . . . old men's tales of an earlier visit . . . a bit of woolen clothing . . . a bit of brass . . . an iron kettle. . . .

At Louisbourg, on Cape Breton Island, a swivel gun of European manufacture and apparent pre-Columbian design was dredged up from the harbor bottom some years ago. The weapon, fired from a socket on a ship's rail, is a breechloader; those who assume that the history of guns or anything else is a steady progression from fist clubs to pistols, or from muzzle loaders to breechloaders to rockets, are regularly open to surprises.

The Conquistadors, on their first landing in Yucatán in 1517—it had taken the Spanish that long to inch across the Caribbean—were met by fierce opposition. It was inspired, they found later, by one Gonzalo Cuerrero, "a seaman of Palos," survivor of a shipwreck, who had been living with the natives for six years. He was tattooed, married, the father of sons, content with his lot, and aware that his adopted civilization must fight or die. It did both.

Two years' later, when Hernando Cortés approached the city of Mexico, Montezuma's ambassadors borrowed a soldier's helmet to compare with one left by the ancestors who had long before predicted the coming of men with beards from the east, a relic enshrined at their capital. So says Bernal Díaz, who was there; the helmets must have matched, for the prophecy stood, and made the bloody work of Cortés that much easier.

When eastern Long Island was settled by Englishmen who had been in Massachusetts for one and two decades, the Spaniards had been rulers of Mexico for a century and a quarter. The news of their conquest must have percolated north as easily as did three of the Drake and Hawkins freebooters, English seamen stranded in Mexico in 1568. They walked to Cape Breton Island, at the north end of Nova Scotia, clear across what was to become the United States, and eventually found passage home.

By that date the Spanish had penetrated far into the continent in the south and west. Not many years after the English had established settlements in New England and on the East End of Long Island, the French sphere of influence had expanded from Canada to the Spanish territory of New Mexico and Texas, half a continent away. Except for the far Northwest, where there may have been contact with the Japanese long before this period, the European presence had been felt, if only at second hand, over all of the North American continent by the time Long Island was settled.

The European influence was, in fact, to North America what famine, drought, or pestilence had so often been to Asia—a force setting a continent into political and social motion. Wars, turmoil, and disease went ahead of the white man like ripples across a pool. For the Indians, the European settlement was only the second act of a long tragedy; the curtain had gone up some generations earlier when, at the end of the peaceful and long-extended overture of aboriginal occupation of the land, a lookout's gaze from the masthead of a European ship was returned from the shore.

Chapter
III

IF EUROPEAN MAN FIRST SAW Long Island from the sea, he
came to know it better from the bay side, as had the Indian. The
whites came gradually, as no doubt had the Indians, but they
came over a few decades, while the Indian advance was a matter
of millennia. The whites came by ships and boats, through the
safety of the bays and sounds, to Long Island, for there is no
anchorage on the Atlantic for the whole length of the Island's
South Shore from Coney Island to Montauk Point. On all the
coasts of North America, the availability of proper harbors influenced the pattern of settlement. There are inlets here and
there along the hundred miles and more of the South Shore
that lead to Great South Bay, and Verrazano probably saw
them, but they would have been unsafe for even the smallest
ships of that day. Nautically speaking, Long Island faces away
from the Atlantic, and indeed the commercial fishermen using
its north-facing harbors still refer to it as The Backside.

The Hollander Adriaen Block sailed from Manhattan up the
Sound in 1614, and by the time the island between the North

and South Forks of Long Island had been settled by the adventurer Lion Gardiner twenty-five years later and named Gardiner's Island, that body of water had become the thoroughfare for what little trade and travel there was along the Connecticut coast and between the English settlements of New England and the Dutch at Nieuw Amsterdam on Manhattan Island. Ffarret, a land agent for the Earl of Stirling, who had been granted a near-empire in the New World by James I, was living on the North Fork before Gardiner came to his island; Great Gull Island, a sand pile at the entrance to the Sound, may already have been a European fishing station; and Montauk was known to the Dutch as Vischer's Hoek—Fisher's Point.

The settlers of Long Island, wandering offspring of the Massachusetts' Puritans, half a generation out of Kent, Dorset, Sussex, and the western part of England, came down from New England by water, landing at Southampton from Peconic Bay in 1640 after an impolite exchange with the Dutch at the West End of Long Island, which had been their first choice of "Plantation." The East End Towns—Southampton, Southold and East Hampton—looked north to Connecticut for legal guidance and protection, for they were independent colonies in the beginning, an encroaching nuisance to the Hollanders, who had been trading in Manhattan and the Hudson Valley for nearly half a century. This northerly orientation continued into the twentieth century; there are still East End families with Connecticut "connections" dating back to the days when it was easier to do business by steamer to Hartford than it was to journey by horse and stage, or later train and ferry, to Manhattan, an echo of the explorer's approach by water. So today, cities along the Mississippi half a thousand miles apart feel a kinship for each other that is lacking for the much closer metropolis facing east across the Appalachians.

Long Island's first English settled the South Fork, huddling in villages laid out a half mile and more back from the threatening sea, never forgetting that their way to the rest of the world was through the bays and sounds to the north. They knew, however, that even if trade could not get across the ocean beaches, raiders might—no small consideration in an age when Moorish pirates in the Bristol Channel were coming ashore to

HOOK POND AND THE BEACH BANKS, 1890s

kidnap and loot in western England. This was the period when piracy was to increase for another half-century before it reached its peak, and when, since the great nations were at war a large part of the time, it was often difficult to distinguish between it and their naval operations.

The Indians were generally peaceable at first, and then, as the implications of their position dawned upon them, kept in check by laws controlling their supplies of powder, shot, and rum. As the Indians were tamed they were renamed. In the East Hampton Town records for 1683, a whaler signs an indenture for a season's work off the beach; he is "Hector, alias Akeatum." Another whaler was Awabetom, variously Wabetom or Wobeton; his name occurs many times in the records, in his later years as a gin-keeper, the watcher of a cattle enclosure. His son is simply John Indian, and John's indenture to Richard Stratton in 1683 includes the last mention of his father. Wobetom's grave near East Hampton was excavated in 1917; with his bones was an English bottle, "Wobetom" scratched on its shoulder. Whatever liquor it contained, it was apparently his favorite possession.

Wobetom and his bottle were buried, and dug up, at a spot we would say was near Spring Close Highway just outside East Hampton Village in the Town of East Hampton on the South Fork of Long Island, in Suffolk County, New York. Wobetom, if he thought in such terms, was a chiefling of the Montauk tribe, or band, an Algonkin living on an island he probably called a bastard-Dutch word or words sounding to English ears like Sewanhacky, place of the seawands, the whelk spiral used in the making of white wampum. Although by the time of Wobetom's death toward the end of the seventeenth century he had seen his tribe dwindle to a fraction of the numbers it had had in his youth, the Long Island Indians were far from gone, nor are they yet. Wobetom no longer has a grave of his own, but the land is still his, unless a scant three hundred years of European occupation can be said to outweigh twenty or thirty times as much inhabitation by a people who was not only on the land, but of it.

How long was the land the Indians'? The earliest proven date is a carbon 14 reading of some bones, stained with red ochre in a manner common to ancient North American burials and found in some ancient graves in Europe as well. The date, 1290 B.C., plus or minus 390 years, is for a grave on Sugar Loaf Hill on the glacial moraine at Southampton. It is similar in date and contents to graves on the North Fork some twenty miles away. These graves are not matched by evidence of occupation of the land at that date and have therefore reinforced the belief of some archaeologists and anthropologists that Long Island was for many years visited by the Indians only for burial—a common use of offshore islands facing the rising sun—and that in later days it was occupied only during the warmer months, and then sparsely. Perhaps; no one knows for sure, and it may be that a gradually rising sea has obliterated evidences of early coastal settlements. Whatever the truth, the Indian presence is at least 3,300 years old, which represents great antiquity in human terms if not in geological.

Long Island itself is young geologically, and in its present form does not predate Wobetom's provable ancestral inheritance by a great deal. But if Wobetom haunts this land, as his brethren do our nation, his and theirs are only the primal spirits, the first presences among many. Our country, like our world, was shaped by varied peoples and forces. In the small compass of the South Fork of Long Island, it is somewhat easier to trace the workings of these people and forces than in a nation or continent, but the rules by which they operate hold for large as well as small.

Chapter IV

LONG ISLAND'S IS A LANDSCAPE that makes dunes seem like hills, and hills like mountains. Looking north from Bridgehampton, a farming and resort village in Southampton Town, some ninety miles east of Manhattan, the glacial moraine, rising a scant 200 feet above sea level, looms like a distant mountain range. The hills of the moraine here, a few miles east of Sugar Loaf Hill with its ancient red-ochre burial, are wooded and slope steeply to the fields pushing against their south face. To their north, a tangle of humps and hollows descends gradually toward Peconic Bay; across the bay is the North Fork, and beyond that, Long Island Sound and Connecticut.

But the view from Bridgehampton is toward the Atlantic, for the hilltops are covered with scrub oak, pitch pine, and laurel, blocking the northward gaze. Just below, the ground drops away abruptly and briefly to the south. The boundary of the forest, for which Edge of Woods Road west toward Southampton was named, is abrupt, cutting between the thin sandy soil of the moraine and the fertile ground of the fields below. The fields are the outwash plain of the last great glacier, and their easy slope is barely perceptible.

From this edge of woods, the steeples of the Bridgehampton churches gleam white against the village trees. The fields are divided geometrically by color, brown, green, or yellow according to crop or state of cultivation, and less mathematically by strips of brush and second-growth woods along the gullies and hedgerows. In the haze under an overcast afternoon sky two ponds, Mecox Bay and Scuttlehole Pond, gleam a dull white. Beyond the last fields and the low line of the beach banks at the far end of the long gentle slope, the great waiting ocean is hard to distinguish from the sky, not much more than a darkening of the haze. The landscape does its magnifying trick, and a mourning dove swaying on a telephone wire looms like a hawk.

In the haze, even the bulk of the Woolco store and the Plaza East Shopping Center at the western end of Bridgehampton are hard to make out. Set down into the landscape, out of sight in its hollow across the busy Montauk Highway from the shopping center and the drive-in movie, is Kellis Pond. Kellis Pond is a kettle hole, the last in a line of seven stretching southeast from Shorts, or Scuttlehole Pond, which is in sight, gleaming muddily just below the moraine, cedars growing from its shallows. Kellis and Shorts and their fellows—Haines, Goldfish, Long, Little, and one which might be called Littler Pond but has no name and is visible although nearly overgrown with brush just west of the drive-in—are the work of that last glacier, which receded from Bridgehampton and Long Island perhaps 12,000 years ago, leaving the moraine, the Ronkonkoma, named for the mid-island lake that is the largest of the kettles.

Kettle holes may be formed by great blocks of ice or frozen debris melting away within a glacier's frontal mass of gravel and rock; sometimes they are the work of runoff water from the glacier. Some kettles nurture swamps; the North Neck kettle at

Montauk is of this sort, a peaceful place of bull brier and swamp maple, warblers and raccoons. Others, like Kellis, hold ponds, often deep. Contrary to tradition, these ponds are never bottomless (the Geological Survey's quadrangle maps show Kellis as containing a modest thirteen-foot abyss) and they hardly ever conceal treasure. The kettles are steep-sided, Kellis almost unbelievably so, given the passage of time and the nature of its surrounding soil. One day in early March when the air was warm, snow lay deep on the northwest side of the pond. In the shade of the abrupt bank, the drifts blown there by the winds of January and February were perhaps the only snow left on all of Long Island that day, a small echo of the melting glacier ice 120 centuries before.

The historian James Truslow Adams, who pondered Bridgehampton's past before going on to the nation's, wrote in his *Memorials of Old Bridgehampton* that the name Kellis was not Indian, as some supposed. The pond was named, he said, for one John Kelly, "who was early allotted land there."

"Kellis Pond used to drain into Mecox Bay through the canal-like depression still clearly marked, running in a southwesterly direction," Adams wrote. The Geological Survey contour maps trace a stream running from the pond into Calf Creek, shown as a streak of blue passing under New Light Lane, which was named for the church built there in 1748, a consequence of the great schism in the East End church, then the only church, later the Presbyterian. The New Light reformation of the Reformation itself precipitated the retirement from the ministry of one of my ancestors on the pious side, Nathaniel Huntting, East Hampton's second pastor, an old-breed cleric who quit his post in 1746, after fifty years in that ministry. There is no trace of a church on New Light Lane today, unless one counts that modern shrine, the heavily glassed summer house. Several such are in evidence in a landscape also graced by the milk-bottle shape of a radio beacon, which guides executive Lear jets to East Hampton Airport each Friday afternoon and back out Monday morning.

The beacon is not far from the head of navigation on Calf Creek, by the Mecox Road bridge. Calf Creek is no Blue Nile; it runs dry only a few hundred yards upstream. Following the gully toward its source, one comes to a subdivision road running straight toward Kellis Pond between twin rows of new houses, each no doubt with its family membership in the conservationist Group for America's South Fork. The houses parallel the one-time stream, and the road ends in a turnaround just short of Kellis Pond, which, at a guess, would have to rise two or three feet over its bank, which is low here, to run out toward Calf Creek along what is now more like a wide hedgerow than a stream bed. The dry channel is perhaps forty feet across, with the shoots of tiger lilies showing green in early spring among the usual hedgerow black cherries and beer cans. Across the pond, to the northeast, is a matching gully, wider and full of water, pointing up toward Bridgehampton, where it becomes Snake Hollow and skirts the shopping center, to which an adventurous management might have given its name.

Exploring southeast from the Calf Creek dreen (to use a South Fork pronunciation of the noun "drain") a dreen that no longer dreens, one finds a considerable swamp. If Calf Creek were the Blue Nile, this would be the Sudan. On its far side a small caravan of wrecked cars and a derelict red-and-white oil dealer's truck has congregated. A one-room shack droops in a beech-shaded hollow by the swamp, its front wall gone. Within are the remains of an iron bedstead, a kerosene stove and an ice box. If it was once occupied by one of Bridgehampton's up-from-the-South farm hands, the shanty's surroundings must have reminded him of home. This is a possum swamp, a weasel swamp. A friend of mine who knows his animals swears he once found an otter's tracks on the banks of Kellis Pond. On the first day of spring, there were teal and black duck on its waters, red-winged blackbirds singing in the bushes by the narrow sandy beach that stretches between the swamp and open water at the lower end of the pond, and evidences of seasonal lust to be seen where youngsters park after a trip to the drive-in, at the upper end.

Down toward the ocean, the fields stretch away for miles on either side. The South Fork magnifier is at work again, and the sky becomes a great dome. To the west, equestrians from Swan Creek Farm bob in silhouette against the haze over Mecox Bay. To the east are rows of elms. On that first day of spring, the fields were still brown with the winter's cover crop. Plowing was about to begin, and at the barn on the Horsemill Lane corner, men were mending equipment. The small pond behind the barn was dotted with ducks. A flock of Canada geese and a straggling of gulls watched from the field beyond. Shorebirds picked at the wet ground running down to the pond. Two cars were stopped by the lane, each with its telescope for bird-watching clamped to the passenger-side window. At the end of the lane, the brackish sheet of water called Mecox Bay was whipped into froth along the shore by a brisk southwest breeze. Off to the left were Swan Creek and Sam's Creek, the houses on the beach banks along Dune Road, and the low land between Mecox Bay and the second body of spring-fed water, Sagaponack Pond. This, Adams wrote, was all swamp once. Now it is fertile farmland, spotted with houses old and new. Two more are going up across from the Mecox Cemetery. They are modern, but their architect's mother must have been frightened by a saltbox. They look toward the Atlantic.

Across the winding road called Job's Lane, the headstones in the cemetery turn their backs on the Atlantic and the new houses and face toward the distant moraine. The inscribed names are repeated again and again in the land all around: Sandford, Tal-madge, Howell, Hedges, Cook, Osborn, Halsey, Sayre. The older stones are at the west end of the burying ground, far from the road. Some of them, made of dark slate, are well preserved. Newer sandstone markers have not worn as well.

Chapter

V

EAST AND WEST OF THE Mecox Cemetery, potato ground—fine sifted-down soil from the glacier, rich with the humus of 120 centuries, which was swamp bottom not so long ago—tilts gently toward the sea, turning up abruptly at the dunes and then dropping down once more onto the beach. Behind the dunes, much of the land is below ten feet in elevation. The soil continues under the dunes, to be exposed along the beach by storms and washed away as the ocean advances. Adams reports that a line of fence posts, which from evidence in the Southampton Town records may have dated back to the late 1600s, once reappeared on this stretch of beach two centuries later. After a violent three-day northeasterly gale in March 1962, ancient cart tracks and the hoofprints of oxen were found on the beach here and at the village beach of Wainscott to the east, imprinted on broad surfaces of freshly exposed peat. The peat was pond bottom in Colonial times; the dunes, moving landward, have crossed the southerly boundary of the settlers' fields and the ponds of that time, leaving the ancient cropland and peat under the beach sand.

This is a landscape where small looms large, but it was not always so. Once the landscape was truly large enough for any eyes. From the moraine north of Kellis and Scuttlehole ponds, as the great glacier melted away, retreating back along a line extending from New England through the Midwest, some 12,000 years ago, the Atlantic shore was over the horizon to the south, a good sixty or seventy miles distant. The land simply sloped away from hills, which were then some 650 feet above sea level. In those days, a good deal of the world's water was stored away in glaciers, and the seas were perhaps 430 feet below their present levels. They have been rising ever since; the present rate is about one foot per century.

The oceanfront ponds, Mecox, which is really not a bay at all, and Sagaponack and Georgica, are not kettle holes, but low areas blocked off by sand bars, catch basins for rainfall. Given the sea's rate of rise, a little one, like Fairfield Pond east of Saga-ponack, may be merely the surviving northern tip of what was a much larger pond when the whites arrived on this landscape, a pond made small by the rising Atlantic and its attendant dunes. Our Sagaponack Pond may have been, when the Indians arrived, to a larger pond what Calf Creek now is to Mecox.

Each winter Mecox Bay freezes, sometimes early, at the end of November or in early December; sometimes later, in January. Most years there is ice enough—three, four, six, even fourteen and eighteen inches at times—for iceboating. There may be only a day or two of sport before a heavy snow spoils it; sometimes it lasts for weeks on end, even for a month or two. The boats, old jib-headed stern-steerers, modern bow-steerers, and scooters, duck-boats without a steering runner which are directed in their hurtling course by manipulation of the jib, are dragged down from barn lofts by living members of the families in the cemetery nearby, by Halseys and Toppings and Hildreths, and brought to Mecox. Like their fathers and grandfathers before them, these men are mostly farmers. Their harvest is in, the cover crop is planted, and spring is far away. If the weather and the ice hold, they will iceboat day after day while others toil in office, store, or factory. Those among them who have such jobs find ways to take time off.

Despite long spells of freezing weather, Mecox and the other coastal ponds rarely freeze entirely. There are usually holes, large ones, kept open by springs and the paddlings of the ducks and geese which rest by the open water all day long, moving from the surrounding fields at dawn and returning at dusk, taking off to circle in gabbling flight when an iceboat comes too close. The boats, traveling faster than the wind itself at forty, fifty and sixty miles an hour, rumble like trains when the ice is dry and hard. When the frozen surface is topped by a little water, at the end of a sunny day or after a shower, the ice is at its fastest, and the boats sizzle along. At times this thin slick of water will itself freeze at its surface, and drain away through holes or evaporate in the dry winter air, leaving a delicate layer of white ice a quarter inch above the gray-blue of the true surface. An iceboat, crashing across an acre or two of this, sounds like a giant tearing at a circus tent, or a bullet crashing through a series of chandeliers.

None of these sounds, however, can be heard over the mile or two from which the boats can be seen across the winter landscape, speeding along silently, their sails white pyramids moving above the intervening fields where stubble and winter wheat poke through the snow, snow that is deep only in the lee of hedgerows and fencing.

At the end of the day the iceboaters stand by their pickup trucks, boats resting off the ice on small sawhorses, runners removed and packed in boxes to be sharpened that night at the workbench in the cellar for tomorrow's sailing, and sip cocoa or brandy. They talk about the sailing, and when a pair of black duck passes overhead, someone puts his mug down and raises his arms as if they held a shotgun, swinging on the birds. Another iceboater laughs and says, "Too far! Too far!" The cadence is quick, the intonation lifting. It is the speech of his father, and his father's father's father.

Sagaponack Pond, two miles across the fields to the eastward, was compared to a river by Peter Matthiessen, who lives near it, in his book *The Wind Birds*. Sagaponack twists north to Poxabogue Pond, which is, like Kellis, a kettle hole, and, again like Kellis, the southernmost in a line of kettles, this series running almost due north to Sag Harbor, a line punching clear through the Ronkonkoma moraine.

Matthiessen's wind birds are the sandpipers, the plovers, all the quick wild waders and striders of the South Fork beaches, flats, and bars when they are not two or three thousand miles to the north or south. Great travelers, they were hunted once, like the ducks and geese today with which they share these ponds and creeks in season. In the spring, freed from the ice which usually traps them before the end of the fall hunting season, the floating blinds are dragged up from Mecox and Sagaponack and rest, their gray or khaki paint peeling, their reed camouflage tattered, in the farmyards beside the sharpies, the flat-bottomed skiffs used for crabbing, eeling, oystering, or gill netting on the ponds. South Fork farmers remain the amphibious creatures their ancestors were. Within living memory, those champion potato growers, the Osborns of Wainscott hamlet, killed a whale offshore, and from a little dory at that. Most of the family names in the Mecox Cemetery can be found on the long roster of the Sag Harbor whaling captains, but with farming now big business, some of the descendants have no time for the pursuit of pond perch, let alone whales.

Even in the old days, however, fishing and whaling rarely approached farming as a source of income in this corner of Long Island. Go back up to Scuttlehole Road, where the fields begin on the south side of the moraine above Water Mill and Bridgehampton. Adams repeats an old story concerning the name:

A peddler, whose wagon had mired in a slough up there, was asked how he got it out. "Oh," he said, "I had to scuttle to do it." Now, Adams was no nay-tive, or he might have known better. A scuttlehole was the East End's widow's walk, a trap door behind the ridgepole of a saltbox house, from which one could climb out to extinguish a chimney fire, or gaze out to sea. However committed to farming, the South Fork countryman continues this seaward study as a daily ritual.

From Scuttlehole, Bridgehampton's ridgepole, the view is always toward the Atlantic, south over thousands of acres of farmland, the famous Bridgehampton loam. Farmed intensively for three centuries now, it would support some of its families for another three if it could be saved from subdivision and paving for tennis courts and driveways. The soil slopes gently, dropping perhaps 150 feet in two and a half miles between moraine and ocean beach. The landscape's chief characteristic is its flatness, the smoothness one would expect in an old, old landscape. Yet this is a new landscape, formed yesterday in terms of geologic time. Only here and there, in the incline of the banks of Kellis Pond, for example, are there the rough edges to be expected in something new, but new it is in the world's scale. The land's components have made its smoothing easy; if they had been granite, the South Fork landscape would be all rough edges. Instead, the earth here is made up of sands and gravels and silts and soils, materials easily transported, layered, rounded, smoothed, and finally flattened into a gentle contour under a domed sky at the edge of a broad gray sea.

The shape was there long ago, but man has made his mark.

The native Americans may have arrived not long after the land was rough-shaped by the glacier while it was still unsmoothed. There is no archaeological evidence of their presence on Long Island so early, but they were no doubt in North America even before that time. We can guess that the early inhabitants of Long Island, like their counterparts today, demanded waterfront property, and in those days Long Island Sound would have been a great hollow or a lake; Long Island was no island, and the ocean beach was far away by the edge of the Hudson Canyon, the great present undersea extension of the Hudson River's bed. Did the first inhabitants cluster there, feasting on drift whales and keeping a wary eye out to their rear for mastodons? Whatever the date of his arrival, the red man was here for a long, long time and left little mark upon the land. Or did he?

Hempstead Plain—the largest prairie east of the Mississippi, before its conversion into the Roosevelt Field shopping center, the Nassau County Coliseum, tract housing, and parkways—was, some believe, man-made, a tract of land cleared by burning long ago for crops or easier hunting. The early Long Island records are full of "little plaines," "great plaines" and "meadows," many of them apparently in existence when the white men appeared. Amagansett, the resort village just east of East Hampton Village now favored by the singles crowd, had its Indian Wells Plain, and Montauk its Ditch Plain and Hither Plain; Bridgehampton itself was built upon "the Brushy Plaine." Eastern Long Island was well-wooded, too, according to the records, but these open areas, most of them in places with excellent soil, ought to have been covered by trees unless something interfered. Were the plains cleared by girdling of tree trunks, or burning, or both, by the Indians? When the English arrived, the Indians were not numerous enough to have required fields of this extent.

Yet we have no sure idea of what the native population had been a century earlier, before the white man's diseases, which preceded the white man's settlement in a convenient and, some believed, providential manner, diminished the red man's numbers. Gardiner's Island was Manchonake—the Island of the Dead —when Lion Gardiner arrived there in 1639, and uninhabited. By that date, the Long Island Indians had been thoroughly exposed to smallpox, diphtheria, and measles by a long procession of explorers, seamen, and real estate agents.

There is no one left to tell us whether or not the great and little plaines were Indian gardens. The Montauks and Shinne-cocks remaining do not speak their ancestral language, and after three centuries of our occupation, little is left of a history that was always oral. The best and oldest evidence of our past is in the land itself, and that still slopes down from the moraine past Bridgehampton and Mecox toward an ancient sunken beach.

Chapter VI

IN THE LAND, the oldest of the formal cemeteries on the South
Fork is at Indian Field, Montauk, where lie the bones of Montauks probably dating back to well before the arrival of the
English, and dating forward to the early years of the twentieth
century. The graves face the midday sun from the slope above
Great Pond, renamed Lake Montauk by the real estate developers
of the 1920s. Bordering the fenced portion of the cemetery
is the only Indian Garden of which we can be 100 percent sure,
today a subdivision of that name, whose residents stare curiously
at Red Thunder Cloud of Three Mile Harbor when he puffs
tobacco smoke to the four winds there each Memorial Day. A
newer subdivision just up East Lake Drive has been named
Indian Rills.

The South Fork has modern cemeteries, too, running to heavy
headstones, perpetual care, and floral blankets, but they are far
outnumbered by the old burying grounds, like the South and
North End cemeteries in East Hampton Village. These two,
until recently, were run by elected trustees, a vestige of the days

when there was no line at all between church and state on the Puritan East End, and so far as I know contain not one certifiable Indian, either Christian or heathen.

The cemetery trustees' place on the ballot was doomed by the limitations of the voting machines and a conjunction in the Nelson Rockefeller years of various New York State referendums and constitutional questions and vacancies in weightier office; the trustees were pushed off the far end of the ballot. The officers of the nonprofit corporations entrusted with the affairs of the ancient cemeteries are now self-perpetuating; they tend to choose as their successors those who, like themselves, can count many ancestors among their tenants.

The old church-oriented public cemeteries are in turn out-numbered by the family burial grounds. The Lesters at Round Swamp, East Hampton, still inter their dead on the Lester premises. The Terrys, at Northwest Harbor, are all below ground now, and the Town tends the twenty or thirty graves there, keeping the post-and-board fence, one of several dozen such put up during the Depression as make-work projects, in repair and whitewashed, and mowing the grass once or twice a year.

The Terry graveyard, like the Van Scoy graveyard a mile away through the oaks, is well shaded, a place to rest and meditate on a hot day. Although the hollow metal headstone over one member of the Van Scoy family has been pierced by a large-caliber bullet, the quiet of these hidden family graveyards seems to deter vandalism. A mile or two west of the Van Scoys is the Smallpox Cemetery, with a single marked grave. There was a pesthouse here after the Revolution, far from healthy human habitation between Swamp Road and Northwest Creek; if the pox didn't get you, the mosquitoes would.

They are all gone now: the Indians and the whalers, the Indian whalers, the part-Indians, the part-whalers, the farmer-fishermen, the inheritors of Old Testament tradition and aboriginal planting lore, the narrow, insular men and women who lived and bred and inbred for two and a half centuries in a backwater-corner of the United States, yet sometimes knew Canton or the Sandwich Islands better than they knew New York City. They were human beings with our frailties, although most of them who had major physical frailties were weeded out in infancy. Those who survived—who were often baptized with the name of a departed elder brother or sister, a habit of name-thrifty parents which is the despair of genealogists—were, like ourselves, often wrapped in lives of contradiction.

What sort of people were they? Well, there was Albert Edwards, one of my grandfather's many uncles, a notable killer of ducks, who, in cold weather, would throw off his clothes and paddle out into Great Pond rather than subject his dog to the wet. His brother Joshua, my great-grandfather, once ordered the line cut and a whale abandoned off Amagansett so that he could retrieve his prize sealskin cap, which had been lost overboard in the flurry. The third brother, Gabriel, was knocked unconscious by a whale's flukes and came to days later muttering, "Where's the whale?" I remember my grandfather, as tough as his uncles, clutching a tiny bouquet of Northwest woods maypinks, which other parts of the country call trailing arbutus, in his large scarred fist.

Joshua's wife, Adelia Conklin, broke a pool cue over the backside of her youngest son when he came home, late for the chores, from the Amagansett billiard hall. Her daughter-in-law, Florence Huntting, broke her wrist harnessing a horse to fetch her husband home from cod fishing off the ocean beach one winter night, but never bothered to have it set or even to complain about it and went to her grave sixty years later with a small, thin hand still twisted in arthritic pain.

What kind of people? People incorporating the same mixture of hardness, greed, violence, piety, idealism, and blunt Mark

Twain humanism that characterized most of the westward drive of American civilization. Greed was the prime motivator of that drive, and it certainly marked the settlers' dealings with the Indians, on Long Island and nearly everywhere else. But white-Indian relations on the South Fork of Long Island were notable for the relative absence of violence. Piety surely was present; the notion of separation of church and state never occurred to the early settlers, and the decline of religion as a moving force in day-to-day political and social affairs is relatively recent. And the East Enders shared with their New England cousins and the town builders and the church founders all across the continent the idealism that made Americans conscious of their opportunity to build a new and better order on these shores, and gave them egalitarian dreams and aspirations of a high order. There was blunt humanism too, contradictory as it may seem in a society that for much of its history was church- (and money-) oriented; the freethinkers of the late eighteenth century left their mark even in pious East Hampton, where they formed an infidel society and Stephen Burroughs was Bridgehampton's rakehell version of Tom Paine.

Among my mother's papers there is a folded letter with traces of sealing wax below the address:

> Mr. Gabriel Bennet
> Ship *Thames*
> Southern Hemisphere
> Atlantic Ocean

Per Ship
Nimrod

Amagansett, Sept. 20th 1836
Friend Gabriel—By the request of your Sister I write unto you. Last Sunday we received the melancholly information of the

death of your brother Joshua. He died on the 29th of last May in the City of Rotterdam, the port where the ship was owned. They arrived there only two weeks previous to his sickness, he was sick three weeks with a fever and died. . . .

Yours
H. L. Mulford

P.S. Your Sister Irene would send you a bottle of good cherry wine, but there have been no wild cherries this summer.

In the envelope with this, there is another letter, from Joshua's nephew and namesake, who had been five when his uncle died in Rotterdam. Joshua Bennett Edwards, at his writing, was thirty-one and a whaler too:

Dear Brother and Sister,

. . . We have not seen one sperm whale since last May . . . I have not received but two letters since we left the Western Islands, one from you and Phebe and one from Gabriel but I think there will be some by the next mail . . . I want you should write as soon as you get this. . . .

Consider the address: Ship *Thames*, Southern Hemisphere, Atlantic Ocean! By 1861 Joshua Edwards of Amagansett had whaled in the Atlantic, the Pacific, and the Arctic Ocean, had seen his captain killed by a three-ton blanket piece of blubber in the Bering Sea (and had been slandered with the other ship's officers as having conspired in the death of the master, a hard man), had taken part in the '49 Gold Rush and commanded a coasting schooner between California and Alaska. He was reputed to have thrown overboard a Hawaiian girl, presumably a swimmer, found waiting in his bunk in the anchorage at Honolulu, and he probably knew more about the ports, gulfs and shoals on the other side of the equator than he did about the western reaches of his home county. Four months without a sight of a sperm whale was nothing unusual in the business. A whale might yield fifty barrels of oil; there are said to be millions of barrels of petroleum in the sea bottom off Long Island, for the drilling.

Distance sometimes had less meaning to our ancestors than it does to us, to whom it is a matter of hours, not months. Time weighed differently, too, to people to whom life was but a short span between birth and an eternity which might be spent in heaven or in hell, depending upon one's works and beliefs during life. This promoted extremities of behavior among ordinary people rarely seen today; if one was doomed and knew it, there was not much point in good works; if one reckoned on a fair chance of a pleasant afterlife, there was little profit in risking it.

Some captains would whale on Sundays, others not. There were many Sundays in a voyage four or five years long; and many whalers, Joshua Edwards among them, who would not marry until a career of four or five such voyages was over. Joshua's distant cousin Sanford Edwards was married, however, and along about 1830, when he was twenty-five or so years old, domesticity palled and he disappeared, leaving behind at lonely Barnes Hole, on the west shore of Gardiner's Bay, his wife, Rachel, and their infant daughter, Phebe Ann. As the family may have guessed, he had gone a-whaling. Two years later there was a tap on the bedroom window, and an alarmed Rachel screamed, "Who's there?"

Sanford's voice was calm. "Good evenin', Retchel, how's Phebe Ann do?" Two years was not a voyage calling for elaborate greetings or explanation.

Family stories. Sanford's son, Charles Sanford Edwards, years later, jumped down to a Boston wharf from the deck of a menhaden steamer out of Promised Land, the docks around the beach from Barnes Hole. He was not seen until the next morning.

"Where ye been?" the irritated captain asked. "Just taken a walk," Charles Sanford replied. "And where did ye take this walk?" the captain persisted. "Up three flights of stairs," Charles Sanford admitted; he had not spent the night alone.

Family fights. Charles Sanford, come ashore and living in Amagansett, and his wife, Ede, for many years ate their meals, cooked at opposite ends of the stove, in silence at a table divided down the middle by a board on edge.

My great-uncle Dan Huntting, great-great-great-great-grand-son of the Reverend Nathaniel, spent a long life caring for his beloved horses at the family place in East Hampton and admiring from afar Theodore Roosevelt. He married for the first time at the age of seventy-nine; his bride was his housekeeper, Sadie, a woman in her sixties, and I was the only member of the family willing to go over and congratulate them. Dan was out by the barn, leaning on his pitchfork. "Yes," he said, "I'm glad I waited. Plenty of chances, but I'm glad I waited." I murmured something, and Dan swiped at a stray dribble from a cud of Brown's Mule chewing tobacco before continuing. "Yes, Evvie, you and Florrie have been very happy; marriage can be a good thing."

My grandfather, whose name I bear, had been dead for a decade then. Florrie was Dan's sister, my grandmother.

Dan, who had been waited on hand and foot all his life by his other sister, Minnie, who was not long dead at the time of his marriage, was particular about what he ate. He was engaged in a monologue of food criticism one noon when his exasperated bride-and-cook came up behind him and began to tenderize the top of his head with a length of stove wood. The marriage broke up then and there; Sadie's reported observation was, "Them Hunttings bruise easy." In the wake of their separation, Dan's competency at the time of the ceremony became a legal issue, and one day over at the Court House in Riverhead, Judge L. Barron Hill, gazing mournfully at the portrait of Eisenhower at the back of the courtroom, inquired, "Mr. Huntting, who is the President of the United States?"

"Roosevelt," Dan shot back.

"Which Roosevelt, Mr. Huntting?"

"Teddy, you damned fool," Dan snorted.

His grasp of current events notwithstanding, the marriage,

WHALE ON THE BEACH AT AMAGANSETT, 1890s

annulled by Judge Hill, was made whole again in the Appellate Division. The separation continued, however, and Mrs. Huntting died one afternoon in the Lions Club ambulance of a massive overdose of aspirin.

Dan went on for some years as irascible as ever; his father's double-barreled ten-gauge shotgun with the old rabbit-ears hammers was always leaning in a corner by the kitchen door with a handful of shells ready on the window ledge for horse-chasing mongrels, tramps, coastguardsmen (they rent horses, and gallop 'em on the pavement), and Jehovah's Witnesses (them Jehovahs). Toward the end of his days Dan decided, studying a gunfight scene in his favorite book of Frederic Remington reproductions, to put a large hole in a neighbor. Dan was a premature Rachel Carsonite and had concluded that the DDT meant for the neighbor's apple trees which was drifting over the property line was harmful to his horses. In addition, everyone knew that the boundary had been wrongfully extended onto Huntting property ninety or a hundred years back to take a jog around the woodpile next door in the days when woodpiles, for convenience, were maintained in the front yard. My grand-mother got wind of impending slaughter and hid Dan's shotgun shells, then made the rounds of the hardware stores with orders to tell Mr. Huntting when he came in that they didn't make ten-gauge anymore.

Deprived of his ultimate satisfaction, Dan spent his last days puffing angrily at his pipe in the old easy chair in the southwest bay window, the very spot where his father, Jeremiah, had spent half a century of Sunday mornings telling anyone who would listen of the hypocrisy of his various contemporaries who were entering the Presbyterian church across wide elm-lined Main Street. Dan, between puffs, catalogued the villainies of the Polacks and Eyetalians and Dutchmen to whom the family farm had been sold in installments to support him and his horses. His nurse, a black man, smiled indulgently and continued work on a novel of science fiction as Dan moved on to the iniquities of the niggers, who smelled his kitchen up frying chicken and never poached up any fish for the cats.

Family ghosts. For fifteen years before and fifteen years after the turn of this century, John Wilkes Hedges presided over the

slow decay of the Hedges farm on the outwash plain at Sagaponack. John Wilkes, his countenance twisted by an early stroke,
would read all night in the big house half a mile up from the
beach, the light from his bedroom window visible for miles at
sea, would read all night to the music of his Swiss music box,
eat a breakfast the next noon prepared by his two maiden sisters,
shoot quail in the afternoon with his English shotgun and his
Irish setter Bismarck, ride five miles to Sag Harbor on Saturdays
dressed like a Southern planter, to stand on the sidewalk by the
Savings Bank and tell, as his own experiences, tales from the
midnight novels.

John Wilkes Hedges' sister Esther or Et, was for decades the
secret sweetheart of the hired farm manager, William Mooney
the Irishman. Et died, leaving Mooney half the farm and half the
house, where he died years later, crippled by multiple sclerosis.
Et's sister Ann, who outlived her by a few years, boasted truth-
fully almost to the last that she had never ridden in an automobile, that dretful machine. Cousin Ann, tricked at last into
the back seat to talk with an invalid relative, was carted scream-
ing to Bridgehampton and back. That was in 1931 or thereabouts,
and the work of my grandmother, who relished such foolery.

They are all gone now. Miss Mary Cooper, born in Stoke
Poges, England, raised on Gardiner's Island, who lived in a little
house on the Hedges place and came for the coldest part of each
winter to sew with my grandmother for a month or so, for her
board. Mary Cooper, fat and jolly and smelling like starch,
although her home at Sagaponack always reeked of kerosene.
Mary Cooper, who had caught Et Hedges and her beau, the
shanty Irishman, spooning in the orchard, and did not say a word
until one of those sewing sessions half a century later.

Ghosts and family stories, jumbled in time and place.
Grandma, gone with a team to Montauk, bearing a milk can full
of beef broth and another full of fresh milk, to greet the Rough

Riders coming ashore from the transport *Miami* in 1898, fresh from Cuba. Each trooper, she said, had a toothbrush stuck in his broad-brimmed cavalry hat like a cockade, and the band played "The Battle Cry of Freedom." In all, 29,500 soldiers came to Montauk late that summer, to camp on the hills until they were certified free of yellow fever, typhoid or the effects of profiteers' provisions, and discharged, or buried—263 of the soldiers died there. Theodore Roosevelt, commanding the Rough Riders and the most glamorous if not the senior officer present, made the plans and contacts at Montauk which led him to the presidency. Cousin Theodore Conklin, not impressed by position or shared names, horsewhipped Teddy Roosevelt, Jr., for sliding down his haystack. The boy's father is said to have cried "Bully!" or more likely, "Give it to him!" in approval.

Off Montauk a generation later, Uncle Bert Edwards suspended an officious Coast Guard officer by his collar out over the rail of his beam trawler. It was during Prohibition, and the Coast Guard was said to devote its time to the innocent while turning a blind eye toward the rum-running vessels. Bert's son Herb taking his trawler and his crew of kindred spirits to the amusement park in New London, Connecticut, across the Sound for a long weekend of bibulous frolic as an alternative to toiling on the sea, which he was exceedingly good at when he was in the mood.

Aunts Atalie and Lillian Worthington were frail old ladies whose paternal grandfather had been a private in Washington's army, and aunts only in the sense of older female friends. Atalie, who like her sister had never married, was I suppose in love with my grandfather. The two of them blackberried together in all innocence in their old age on the hills at Montauk. I remember Atalie, in ancient photographs a beautiful maiden, staring with octogenarian eyes at the muscles of one of my stroke-oar friends from college, and Atalie, a lovely woman even when her face was old and wrinkled and salted with white hairs she could not see, sewing for her living with her work held an inch or so from her nose.

I remember Uncle Gabe Edwards and his cronies snickering in the balcony at the Southampton movie house at the 1930s version of *Moby Dick:* "Wrong, all wrong; they'd all be killed."

Ghosts, memories. My grandmother's great-grandmother Osborne; she died in 1848, and could boast to the end she'd "never used a cookstove." A long life's meals had been prepared over open fires. Joshua Edwards slipped his gold into his boots as the Confederate raider *Shenandoah* pursued the whaler *Jireh Perry* in the Bering Strait. It was 1865 and the war was over, but neither whalers nor Confederates knew it. The *Perry* escaped, and the gold helped put Joshua's third son, David, through medical school decades later.

Indian ghosts, a long procession led by Steve Talkhouse, tall and silent, a symbol to rouse the guilt of those whose ancestors took the land from his, but who knew there could have been no other way. Toward the end of the procession, for my generation, it is Pocahontas Pharaoh, making scrubs—round-handled oak splints bound and split at the end to use as kitchen brushes—at museum demonstrations, or in buckskins and beads at the East Hampton Ladies Village Improvement Society Fair.

Steve Talkhouse, sold to Colonel Parsons as a boy for a dollar a pound; forty-dollar Steve Talkhouse, who walks the land still in our recollection of Long Island as it was or might have been; Steve Talkhouse, Civil War veteran, coming up through the snow from Hither Wood to Second House at Montauk, blood streaming from a bone-deep ax cut in his foot. He asks Mrs. Stratton to fill the wound with rock salt. Mrs. Stratton, faint, turns to Mrs. Cartwright, who calmly pours the salt. Steve pulls his stocking up over the wound, puts his gashed shoe back on, and strides away, walking still, from Rod's Valley on the west shore of Fort Pond Bay through the beeches, oaks, and laurel to Napeague and Bridgehampton and Sag Harbor and Brooklyn and back; he'll do your errand, take your message, for two bits.

Ghosts in all the families, white, black, red, and in between. The new families, here for a century and more at the time of my boyhood and in many instances more appreciative and understanding of their surroundings than the old-timers, are dimmer in my memories than those people of two centuries back known through the family stories, those figures dead in the little cemeteries behind white fences, yet alive in a tradition more real, more a part of the remembered landscape of my growing up than the city people driving golf balls across that landscape.

TODAY'S CITY PEOPLE, many of them graduates of Manhattan reform Democratic politics, are likely to imagine themselves set down in a wilderness inhabited by Republicans of the most un-regenerative stripe. In fact, the newcomer is surrounded by relics of Democratic politics almost as ancient as Tammany itself.

My maternal grandfather, born six years after the Civil War, voted, like most of his family and perhaps a majority of his cousins—a category that in its broader sense, until about the time of his death in 1950, included perhaps half of the people of the South Fork—for the second Roosevelt three times.

He never, so far as I know, repeated the 1944 slogan of coarse-minded Republicans: Three times is enough for any man. Grandpa was raised on a farm, but nonetheless was something of a prude. One night a year or two before that election of 1944 when he decided that Roosevelt, Democrat or not, had been in office long enough, I heard an exchange of whispers from the front bedroom at my grandparents' house. I was staying in the room just behind, my habit when I was angry with my own family and one to which no one seemed to object.

Grandpa, *sotto voce*: "They's banned *Esquire* magazine from the mail. Too dirty."

Grandma, apparently unshocked: "Tssssk."

She sang a different song one night a few years later when Grandpa, dreaming, was at the steering oar guiding a dory or whaleboat through a heavy surf. His stroke oar turned his head to look over his shoulder at an approaching breaking sea, a grievous and most dangerous error, and roaring "Eyes in the boat!," Grandpa swung for his jaw. Grandpa was squaw-handed, left-handed, and Grandma always slept on his right. His left fist caught her on the left side of her face, and Grandma, a tiny woman, was knocked out of bed, falling between its side and a cast-iron radiator. Thus forewarned, when she heard the shout "Eyes in the . . ." a few months later, she slid fast toward the foot of the bed, and Grandpa's fist smashed against the radiator. He never dreamed that dream again.

Nor did he, I think, vote for Truman in 1948. By that time he had forgiven me for carrying a literal torch for Wendell Willkie in 1940, in what must have been one of the last torch-light parades in American political history. Up Newtown Lane in East Hampton Village we went, and sang "God Bless America" standing beside the folding chairs on the high school basketball court. My father, raised in California as a Jack London semi-Socialist, had by that time become a conservative Republican, a bit suspicious of Willkie as left of Herbert Hoover, under whom he had served in Russia when Hoover was directing American relief operations during the first famine in the Ukraine. To him, the progression was obvious: the Democratic Party, Socialism, Communism, and cannibalism, whose literal evidence he had photographed in southern Russia, grisly evidence still in the family archives in a locked box.

For my grandfather's family and others on eastern Long Island, and indeed in many agrarian areas of nineteenth-century United States, the issues were different. They believed in free trade and had little sympathy for Lincoln, although many of them fought and died in the Union Army. Here, religion still touched politics; many of the Presbyterian ministers on the South Fork of Long Island were Princeton-trained under a faculty dominated by men raised in the South. They were called Old School Presbyterians, as opposed to the New School Abolitionists, and they must have influenced their congregations. There were Republicans, of course, but the Democratic element among the farming and fishing families remained strong until the days of Franklin Roosevelt, when, ironically, one of the solidest GOP blocs on Long Island, as elsewhere, went the other way, and turned Democratic. This was the black vote; there are long-established black families on Long Island who still remember Abraham Lincoln and vote his party, just as there are old white families who are more conservative than their Republican neighbors but vote Democratic because their daddies and their granddaddies did. They don't think much of Roosevelt, though; Harry Truman, or perhaps George Wallace, is their idea of a Democrat.

Chapter
VIII

POLITICS WAS IN THE AIR in 1876 in Wainscott and Sagaponack, which alone among the East End villages of Long Island are still today much as they were. Separated by low dunes from the ocean beach, they are small farming communities among the great fields of the outwash plain, and the scattered modern weekend homes that have been built are generally unobtrusive. If you approach Wainscott from the north on a night when the wind is blowing clouds from the west across a half-moon, the sea is visible beyond the scattered houses and higher-looming elms, and the sky stretches off toward infinity above. Man is dwarfed by nature. If it is so now, it was more so a century ago. A diary kept in the Centennial year by Oliver Sayre Osborn of Wainscott gives a sense of the life there then, indeed of the lonely farm life that most of the nation led.

Gore Vidal is far from alone in considering the third year of the depression following the Panic of 1873 a year to remember. His novel *1876* focuses on the presidential election, which was won by the Democrat Tilden in the popular vote but was given to the Republican Hayes by a congressional commission. There are political theorists who see this as a sellout and the beginning of a quiet divide-the-spoils understanding between the rural Southern Democrats and the industrialist Republicans of the North which persists to this day.

Oliver Osborn was a Tilden man. In his diary he noted that "election day was a rainy day but all Wainscott went and all but three voted the Democratic ticket. Mr. Talmage and we joined horses and took his carriage. I voted the Democratic ticket strait."

Now twenty-three years old, he had of course been too young to fight in the Civil War, but like most of his fellow Wainscotters, perhaps a hundred or a hundred and fifty of them, mostly related in one way or another, he was a War Democrat—Democrat in politics, but opposed to slavery, a loyal Unionist.

The war had been over for eleven years, but federal troops remained in some Southern states, and as weeks passed after the election and no decision was reached, there was talk of the Southerners rearming, ready to renew the war if Tilden did not take the office they felt was his. Wainscott, however, remained calm, despite its Democratic sympathies. Sagaponack, just west along the outwash plain and over the line in Southampton Town, may have been more restive. Some of its Democrats were said to have flown the Stars and Bars during the late Rebellion, although then as now Washington hardly trembled when Sagaponack grumbled.

Oliver Osborn had yet to marry and was living at home with his widowed mother. He died at eighty-one, and is remembered as an upright man whose seeming gravity hid a love of quiet jokes. He was serious, though, when he wrote in his journal on the evening of July 4, 1876:

One hundred years this 4th since this Government started and small and weak she was then. She is the strongest nation in the world today. If her sons and daughters will obey the laws that their fathers set for them in another Century they will be far ahead of all the world. I am much afraid that they will not but who can tell, time alone will tell. That will soon pass and the next Centennial will find another age. Altogether a different one walking the earth and I don't know but flying in the air. However, I have kept this 4th enough to last me until the next Centennial if I should live as long. If I do not it's all the same.

Oliver had kept the Fourth with a trip to Greenport on the North Fork with friends, including his future bride, Ruth Hedges, and a sail from there down Gardiner's Bay to Sag Harbor, commercial hub of the South Fork and until a few years earlier a whaling port to rival New Bedford. Custer had been dead at the Little Big Horn for nine days, but peaceful summer went on at Wainscott much as it had for more than two hundred years, since the hamlet's settlement in 1668 by Oliver's ancestor John Osborn. It is all in the journal: "moving fence" to protect crops in rotation from wandering stock, haying, chores, "getting in our oats . . . getting out manure, mowing out ditches, harrowing stubble, and various other things that have to be done this time of the year," hauling seine for menhaden, to be spread on the fields as fertilizer. "The first steamers that I ever knew to do any thing fishing off here came along last week. They did well." They, too, were after the oily menhaden; the date was May 27, 1876, and big business had entered what had been a cooperative enterprise among neighbors. The work continued: cutting corn, chopping firewood, mending boots.

The year was broken, however, by a trip to the Centennial Exposition in Philadelphia. In Wainscott, Oliver wrote, "the all important question is when are you going to the Centennial and how did you like it and what is to be seen there." He went ahead, found rooms for his family, returned to New York, and escorted his mother to Philadelphia. Of all there was to see, progress most impressed the young Wainscotter: "I always did like to see machines run and here was a cloud of wheels and belts running and all kinds of machines most that you could wish to see and enough to make one tired before he had seen them all." Back home, "the men were husking corn" on Oliver's return, and gave him three cheers.

Centennial aside, it was a round almost as old as time, which Oliver's ancestors in Kent would have fallen into with little hesitation and almost complete recognition. It was tied, above all, to the seasons and their variations. When Oliver Osborn went to Bull Head (the ancient tavern name which he and others often applied to Bridgehampton) to get the mail (the Wainscott people took turns), it mattered greatly to him which way the wind blew, particularly in rain or snow: "I came home pretty quick. And it was before the wind, I did not get wet enough to change my clothes. The rain soon turned to snow and cleared off before morning. Tuesday was quite a pleasant day only the wind blew very hard and took the snow along with it."

There were excitements, and in them, too, the weather played a part to a degree we find hard to comprehend today. On December 17, after relating how "The wind blew some. It blew the top off of my corn crib which was lashed on. It was of stalks, the rope broke and away she went," Oliver caught up with events of December 11. He was often late in his entries, complaining once: "This Journal is getting to be one of the greatest plagues of my life . . ."

Writing six days after the event, he reported:

Monday night a full rigged ship came ashore at Bridge Hampton just west of Mecox lane. She was soon discovered by the boat house crew. They could not do much till morning then they tried to get off in the metallic life boat as the other one was at the Centennial [as an exhibit] and had not got home yet.

They could not get off for every sea that came would go the length of her [the metallic life boat, a modern contraption much in disfavor among the life saving crews] the same as if she had been a log so they went at work and shot a line to her which they had a hard time to accomplish as she lay on the bar. [The shallow water of the bar generally parallels the South Shore of Long Island, with some 200 to 400 yards of deeper water inshore.] They shot two lines and both fell short, then they got the rocket line which was lighter and they succeeded in getting it on deck.

It was said by some one down there that the second mate tried to catch the ball but they stopped him. How near true it is I do not know. After they got a line aboard they soon got a rope and then a hawser which they hauled with their donkey engine, then they took it to masthead and made it fast, and we hauled moderately from the shore. By this time they thought that they could go there with the boat and did so without much trouble and brought the Pilot and five sailors ashore and got filled coming but none of them got very wet. They then bailed out their boat, went out again, brought more of the crew ashore.

Then I came home. It was dinner time. I got something to eat and felt better.

He had lent a hand, as he would have been expected to by the men of the Life Saving Service, all of whom were hired locally and whom he knew.

The vessel was the *Circassian*, bound for New York after a difficult passage from Liverpool. She had picked up a pilot off Sandy Hook some days before, but had been unable to beat into New York Harbor. She was an iron squarerigger, 280 feet long and displacing 1,741 tons, a large vessel for her day. The *Circassian* drew nineteen and three-quarters feet of water, and was carrying an assorted cargo. In addition to her crew of thirty-seven, there were twelve other sailors aboard, taken from the foundering bark *Heath Park* at sea on November 30. The *Circassian* had a curious past. When she was wrecked, she was under British registry, yet she had been an armed vessel of the Union Navy during the late war, after being captured as a British blockade runner into Confederate ports.

Her compass was off, her master said later, and she struck the outer bar off Mecox late in the evening of December 11 in snow and sleet. She was discovered by Samuel H. Howell, on patrol from the Mecox Life Saving Station, just west of the boathouse, which stood at the foot of what is now Ocean Road, an area with one of the most startling assemblages of modern summer house architecture in existence.

Patrolman Howell saw rockets of distress, and fired his Coston signal flare in response. The Mecox lifeboat, launched the next morning, "made seven trips in all, and broke five oars," according to the station log. "We had at this time 42 persons at the Station. We used the mortar and one shot which landed on the ship's deck, made immediate connection by hand line and hawser. In the meantime the tide had fallen off so that we could use the boat so stated above, and filled the boat but once during the day."

That is, as the sea moderated it became unnecessary to use the breeches buoy, which would bring ashore a man at a time, swinging in a canvas seat from the hawser stretched between masthead and beach. The *Circassian's* crewmen and passengers were all brought ashore safely by boat, and on December 14 the Mecox Station's log notes: "The wreck crews left the Station for New York." On December 16, it was logged that the lifesavers had "put the boat and gear in the house with the exception of the hawser and handline still attached to the ship. One pilot boat stood in and anchored one-half mile east of the Station."

A salvage attempt was to be made. In the meanwhile, life went on at Wainscott. The resumed farm rhythm was hardly broken even by Christmas, which Oliver Osborn observed by taking his mare Kate to Strong's blacksmith shop in East Hampton to be sharp-shod for winter ice. "The roads were very icey," so he went along the beach, only to find that "Mr. Strong had so many a head of me that he could not shoe mine so all that I had to do then was to come home which I did with out much trouble."

Christmas dinner was "pork and beans which I ate with a relish then turned to and helped shell corn till they finished." He thought of going to "Bridge Hampton to a ball that was to be there and to the Christmas Tree that the Sunday School was again to have in the church," but finally "came home and done up the chores and sat down and enjoyed the fire without being disturbed with any word so I went to bed in good season. And this is the way this Christmas past." Outside of the cities, the Charles Dickens–Washington Irving holiday which we now accept as ancient tradition had hardly taken hold; Christmas at Wainscott in a depression year had more of Puritanism than of Clement Moore's contemporary "A Visit From St. Nicholas."

The year 1876 had nearly run out. There was time yet in the Centennial, however, for something to happen, something "so bad," Oliver Osborn wrote, "that I hardly know how to describe it." On his return from the Centennial Exposition in Philadelphia earlier that year, he had written in the journal: "So much for 1876. Who knows what will happen in 1976?"

But 1876 was not over. As it ran out, he took up his pen and wrote, on December 30:

It now comes in my way to record one of the worst disasters that ever happened on the Long Island coast to my knowledge. Perhaps the wreck of the *John Milton* [1858] would be considered nearly or quite as bad but to me this seems the worst. It is so bad at any rate that I hardly know how to describe it. Last night I spent the evening at Corneliuses and when I came out to come home the wind nearly lifted me from my feet it was so strong and from the southeast. Pretty soon after I got home I was surprised to hear the wind from the west, and it blew very hard. I got up and went out to the yard to see if the horses and cattle were all right.

I seemed to feel as if something was wrong some where but every [thing] seemed all right. I went in and soon went to bed. I did not sleep very well. In the morning when we were eating breakfast John [his brother] spoke and said he wondered if they had got the ship off yet and said he forgot to look before and this was the first that I had thought of her. I don't know what I said but he never stopped to finish his breakfast but went right up to the scuttle to see.

The view from the scuttle hole in the peak of the Osborn homestead's roof toward the Atlantic and west toward Mecox, two miles away, was broken by few trees. The *Circassian's* masts must have become a familiar sight in the three weeks since the stranding, towering over the beach banks on the horizon.

When he came down he said that he guessed they had got her off for she was no where to be seen so nothing more was said about her. We finished our breakfast and I went to work in the shop but had not been there long before young Joe came in and said that the ship had gone to pieces and 28 or 29 men lost, some of them Indians, and some of the wrecking crew, some of the ship's crew, and four saved. I did not stop to hear much or ask any questions but went into the house and told the folks that I was going to the beach. It was not much work to go to the beach, all I had to do was pick up my feet and the wind would do the rest.

The wind had hauled up a little then but was blowing hard as ever when I got to the beach I thought I would go to the wreck and started that way but met Dave Sherrill and another fellow. They had been there and said that there was not much

DITCH PLAIN LIFE SAVING STATION, 1898

to see. I thought as the wind blew so and drove the sand in my eyes that I would not go. The beach was strewn with barrels and barrel staves, hard bread, pieces of plank, clothes, and every thing that one could think of that pertained to the ship and her cargo. I learned since that the men that were saved were one of the wrecking crew, the first and second mates [the latter was the would-be bare-hands catcher of the line-gun projectile] and the ship's carpenter, and that the ones lost were ten Indians from Shinnecock Neck and that of the wrecking crew and the ship's crew were on board. I do not know their names.

The worst of it was the accident was all carelessness. The people on shore urged them to keep a line on shore or from the shore to the vessel. But I suppose that the boss of the job wanted to get the vessel off and thought if they had a line ashore that as soon as it began to grow rough that the crew would all leave him so he could not have it. So after it got too rough for a boat to get off there was no way for them to get ashore but to swim as the ship was too far to shoot a line from shore, which they tried to do six times and failed.

The wind blew very hard, so hard that no ship could stand it. She had to go to pieces as soon as the steam pumps stopped working. She filled but she was leaking faster than they could pump before they stopped and they had slipped the cable in hopes she would come near shore. She would not and as it was very large tides when it rose it came all over her and drove the men in the rigging. The mate cut a life preserver out of one of the life boats and took it aloft with him so the four that were saved got on it and came ashore and were pulled out by the boat house crew. The rest of them were all drowned and sad it was none of them drove up but I should have thought they would as most every thing else came up.

The master, Richard Williams of Liverpool, and the boss wrecker, John Lewis, probably had more than one anchor laid out to seaward. They no doubt hoped that as the storm approached

—and as experienced seamen they must have known it was on its way—storm tides and swells would lift the vessel off the bar. Pulling against the anchors, using the power of the steam donkey engine on deck and muscle on the capstan bars, they would then get the *Circassian* off.

Or so they must have thought. They could not do it, however, without the help of the sailors remaining aboard from the *Circassian's* crew, or without the work of the hired Shinnecocks, strong young men, among the last left in their tribe. Some had been whalers, skilled harpooners of the breed Melville had celebrated and the Sag Harbor and New Bedford captains so admired.

Captain Williams and Wrecker Lewis, who had by coincidence once commanded the *Circassian* himself, were urged early on December 29 to send them ashore. They refused; the breeches-buoy line had already been unrigged. The sailors and the Indians would be needed to help get the *Circassian* off the bar and to work her afterward at sea in dirty weather. Rum was served out as the storm approached. At seven o'clock in the evening, as the *Circassian* rolled and pounded on the bar but did not come free, a distress signal was sent up, too late. On the beach, according to the log of the Mecox Life Saving Station,

> We at once proceeded to get the gear in readiness to rescue the persons on board. At 8 p.m. everything was in readiness, guns shotted and line flaked out on the beach. The wind suddenly chops around to the southwest with rain and blowing heavily, which brought everything to the leeward and forced us to shift our position. After much time being spent in changing positions and our match failing to burn properly, we succeeded in firing several shots, but got none on board the ship, owing to the darkness of the night and the strong current running along the shore, it would have been impossible to tell whether they had the line or not.

The abrupt veering of the gale from southeast to southwest, which had so surprised Oliver Osborn as he left Cornelius Conklin's house and gave him an uneasy night, made a maelstrom of the surf between beach and bar. A southeasterly gale immensely accelerates the normal westerly set or drift of the current along the Long Island ocean beaches. In a storm the set will run like a river, parallel to the shore, "as fast," the old surfmen say, "as a man can run." The Army Engineers—who have tamed Western rivers with dams, levees, and rip-rap banks; who have drained great swamps as large as Long Island; who battle nature a good deal more of the time than their fellow soldiers of the infantry or artillery combat the nation's enemies— decided in 1958 to take on Old Ocean. They issued a monumental "Cooperative Beach Erosion Control and Interim Hurricane Study" for Long Island, which seems to have no calculations of this longshore current's speed in storms, an omission comparable to strategy against the Mississippi mapped without calculation of the river's velocity. This may explain why the massive stone groins, up to 750 feet in length, along the Long Island coast, which were built in partial compliance with the study's recommendations, have never worked properly. They were intended to control erosion; but, as in Florida and California, the cure has proven worse than the malady. Eddies around these structures caused by the storm flow, which must reach seven or eight miles an hour, have caused massive erosion, and their very presence along the beach has disrupted a balanced system many centuries old.

The set, under conditions such as those of December 29–30, 1876, is a great mass of water in motion, charging to the west along the shore. Then, as the gale's direction shifts abruptly, the awesome force of the wind comes from the southwest, to be immediately locked in battle with the opposing current. The result is chaos, pyramids of breaking, tumbling water rising without plan or regularity, a belt of mad seas impossible for the most skilled surfman to cross. To return to the Mecox Station's log:

> We were obliged to take position full 50 yards back, or close under the sand hill, on account of the extreme heavy sea and full tide, and the ship had hove seaward twice her length, which lengthened the distance to what it was when we first rescued the crew from her. In the meantime, while getting the gear in position, the mainmast fell by the force of the storm, the sea constantly breaking over her.
>
> We could see with the glasses of the station the men in the rigging, but about midnight the tide fell off, and we saw the lights on her decks and the ship still whole, but her decks completely swept fore and aft. This day ends with heavy westerly winds, cloudy weather, and heavy seas.

The flat conclusion of the log entry was as standard as the bland opening description of the next day's entry:

> Saturday, Dec. 30: This day comes in with heavy westerly gales, cloudy weather, and heavy seas running. At, or about, 2 a.m. discovered that the men on board the ship had again been obliged to take to the rigging, the sea again breaking over her. At 3½ o'clock or thereabouts, discovered that she had broken in two, the forepart settling down, head foremost, and the aft part, stern foremost, mizzen still erect and rigging full of men.
>
> At 4 o'clock the mizzen gradually careened over to port, and about 4½ a.m. settles in the water. Soon thereafter, four men were hauled out of the surf, being all that were saved out of 32 persons on board, they previously securing boat's buoy and arranging it with ropes to hold on by. Captain Henry E. Huntting, Superintendent of Life Saving Service, five of crew from Station No. 11 [Georgica, two miles east], five of the surf

crew tending the ship, and many old and experienced men, residents of the place, were present at the disaster.

On January 2, 1877, the Keeper of the Georgica Life Saving Station wrote in his log:

12 (Midnight) Patrol—Mulford west, met Sanford, Baker east, met King, and found a body which lay on the beach just out of reach of the water about one-half mile east from Station. Patrol at once repaired to Station & notified crew who proceeded to the spot and carried the body above highwater mark and dispatched a messenger to inform Supt. Huntting & also to notify the coroner, who upon holding the inquest the body proved to be that of David Bunn, an Indian of Shinnecock (6 feet 1 inch in length), one of the wreckers lost from the ill-fated ship "Circassian."

There is social history in the listing of the dead, who were identified as Captain John Lewis; three engineers of his Coast Wrecking Company, Luke Steelman, Phillips, and Patsy; Captain Richard Williams; James Thurston of Southampton, England; Earns Johnson, of Liverpool, third mate; Thomas Orr, carpenter's master; Keiff, boatswain; Freeman, sailmaker; John Grant, cook; Horatio Johnston, steward; Frank Wright, apprentice; Allan Nodder, assistant; Walter Hedges, assistant; James Scott; A. B. Andrews; Ladugo, and John MacDermott. The more important crewmen, particularly the American and English, were likelier to be remembered by more or less full names and rank; Patsy was probably an Irishman, Andrews was probably Able-bodied Seaman Andrews, and Ladugo was no doubt a Latin of undetermined species.

The ten dead Indians were David, Russell and Franklin Bunn; William, Warren and George Cuffee; John and Lewis Walker; Robert Lee; and Oliver Kellis, who was not, according to James

Truslow Adams, of the Kellis Pond family. Cuffee, however, is one of the few West African names that survived the Middle Passage and remains fairly common in the United States.

"Circassian widow" was a familiar category on the South Fork for the rest of the nineteenth century, although many remarried. One of the widows was my grandmother's cook for many years. The *Circassian*-lost Shinnecocks left many children, too, yet there is little doubt that their death dealt a mighty blow to what was even in 1876 only the remnant of a tribe. East Enders said, perhaps to assuage their consciences, that the Indians aboard the wreck had been drunk. Drunk or sober, it would have made little difference. They were doomed once the decision was made to keep them aboard.

There was a moon that night, and during breaks in the scudding clouds those "present at the disaster" could see from the beach the men in the rigging, and sometimes hear them. The Indians, those in the crowd below the beach banks said, were praying and singing hymns.

Perhaps those Indian victims, whatever their degree of redness or blackness, of an Englishman's greedy gamble, readying themselves for an icy death aboard a former blockade runner to the Slave States in that Centennial year of 1876, the year of an election in which they could not vote (not that it would have mattered, since the vote had been stolen, anyway), sang this hymn, written around the time of the nation's birth by another red man, Samson Occom, a Mohegan wed to one of their Montauk cousins, and like themselves a Christian:

> When to the law I trembling fled,
> It poured its curses on my head,
> I no relief could find;
> This fearful truth increased my pain,

"The sinner must be born again,"
And whelmed my tortured mind . . .

But while I thus in anguish lay,
The gracious Saviour passed this way
And felt his pity move;
The sinner, by His justice slain,
Now by His grace is born again,
And sings redeeming love.

Chapter
IX

THE TIME TO WALK the ocean beach of the Hamptons where Oliver Osborn found the hard bread and pieces of plank, and the midnight patrol found David Bunn's body, is at low tide on the fall or winter afternoon of a clear day with a moderate northwest breeze. Walk west as the beach itself flows west with the set, facing the warming sun, sheltered from the wind by the dunes to your right. Walk near the surf, gentled by the offshore breeze, down where the sand is hard, freshly tide-packed. From here, the dunes will look higher than they really are, an illusion heightened where there are houses on top of the beach banks, windows staring toward Portugal.

On a weekend there will almost always be someone in sight, often accompanied by a dog or dogs, hard to see against the glint, but distinct against the horizon to the east when you turn back. Even in the dead of winter there is life on the beach, but there is death, too, sometimes more of it than life. There are white bones, shells, the ragged feathers of a dead gull here, live gulls there feeding on decaying fish.

When Edward Topping of Bridgehampton shot a drunken British marauder one night during the Revolution, the redcoat commander, Sir William Erskine, came over in the morning from Southampton. "Is that one of your best men?" he growled to others of the detachment, and kicked the body. "Damn him! Take him down to the ocean and bury him below high water mark."

It was on one of those bright beach-walking days in February, when I was a child, that two young men, Amagansett cousins, headed offshore in a dory. One was seated on the thwart, facing aft and pulling a pair of oars. The other was standing and facing forward, pushing the same pair fisherman-style. Four tubs of codfish trawls, long lines with dangling hooks baited with chunks of skimmer clam, were in the bottom of the boat. A small tumbling surf was running, nothing much, with now and again a bigger swell coming in, the wake of a northeast blow of a day or two earlier.

One of the big seas caught the dory on the bow as they crossed the bar, and, breaking, rolled the boat over. The men clung to the sides of the boat, which was floating bottom up, kicking at their hip boots to get them off. Their grip torn loose by the waves, they swam back and hung on again, the dory drifting slowly shoreward. Another roller passed, and they were tumbled again. One of the men found his footing on the bar, in four or five feet of water, and was laughing when a third sea hit. He disappeared. His companion regained the dory, drifted into shoal water, and was dragged ashore limp with cold. The other man's body came ashore a week later, after his father and relatives had unsuccessfully hauled seine for it as they would for bass or bluefish. It is easy to drown in the surf, even in summer; it was not the storm that the deep-water sailors of the age of canvas feared the most, but the shore.

The Atlantic surf was more than a force of natural selection among the South Fork fishermen, many of whom never learned to swim; it was, in the old days, a social and commercial force as well, turning the villages' faces toward the bays and safe harbors. It was and is a geological force. Like the wind and the rain and the great glacier itself, the surf is the complicated end product of a long series of equations, not easily susceptible to prediction, and trailed by the usual superstitions and old wives' tales. The beach is the surf's arena, its sandy place of battle. If the beach is a battlefield, its backing dunes are battlements.

Chapter

X

AND WHAT ARE DUNES doing a half mile and more from the beach, a beach we have been told is moving landward, not seaward? Bonac, the corrupted version of Accabonac, the Indian name for the creek near Gardiner's Bay five miles north of East Hampton Village, has become a familiar label for East Hampton Town generally. In his poem of that name, John Hall Wheelock celebrated it as the Enchanted land, Where time has died; old ocean-haunted land;/Land of first love, where grape and honeysuckle/Tangle their vines, where the beach-plum in spring/ Snows all the inland dunes. . . .

The poet lived until recently on such an inland dune, up off Georgica Road in East Hampton Village, half a mile from the beach and a hundred miles from Manhattan. Can speculation about the origin of such dunes break the spell of his enchanted land? These inland dunes are at their most obvious as the traveler enters East Hampton on the Montauk Highway, the main road to and from New York. Passing the triangular green, or common, known to the old-timers as the Loam Hole, one sees their slopes flanking the highway ahead left and right, looking like low wooded ridges or high hedgerows. The right-hand, or southerly, dune trails along the highway for a few hundred feet, the bank of an obviously man-made cut. Toilsome Lane, the road off to the left, was not so long ago Highway Behind the Lots. Residents there petitioned to change the name to that of the road it joins further on. The original Toilsome Lane may well have earned its sorry sobriquet because of the drifting sand of yet another set of inland dunes.

There is no accounting for taste in geographical names; those who objected to the sonorous Highway Behind the Lots probably did not know that a long-ago resident of Toilsome Lane did not like that thoroughfare's name, either. She wrestled logic to a fall and ruled that the correct spelling was Tyl's Holm, after Tyler Gould, a leading resident. Her etymology matched that of the linguist who insisted that Louse Point, a minor promontory between Accabonac Creek and Gardiner's Bay, was actually named by some errant French explorer, L'Owsay.

Back to the dunes: The range flanking Woods Lane is covered with trees, brush, and a thin layer of soil, but it was not always so. A less regular dunescape, equally wooded, is on the west side of Toilsome Lane. Harry Sleight, who edited the East Hampton Town Trustees' *Journals* for the period 1725–1772, looked back a century and a half later and noted that on

> June 3, 1736 the Trustees offered to give away the Sand Hills, a peculiar formation of dune land, to the northwest of East Hampton settlement. These hills lying between the road leading to Southampton [the Montauk Highway] and the road to Sag Harbor are now prevented from drifting by formation of beach-grass, and there is tradition that beachgrass was transplanted in earliest years of settlement to "anchor" the sand hills; the experiment was tried at Montauk, some years ago during cattle grazing times, and did prevent sands blowing upon and ruining

pasture lands. The offer of the Trustees made in 1748 provided that the person who bought the Sand Hills, or to whom they would give them if no person appeared to offer money for them, should stop the sand.

Just what was done in 1736 the record does not say. But evidently no fee of the land was given; for Journals years later record leasing of the Sand Hills always with a proviso that they should be fenced to prevent the cattle breaking up the very sparse vegetation. Eventually the lands were sold to the Daytons, and in their deed was a clause to effect that they should always keep the hills enclosed with a sufficient fence.

The Sand Hills on the west could be given away more easily today; they cover forty or fifty acres in an area where half-acre house lots are probably worth close to $20,000. It was while making a deep impression on the Sand Hills (a trench for the Home Water Company) that they first made an impression on me. What, I wondered as I wiped August sweat from my sixteen-year-old brow, were such quantities of sand doing a mile or so from the sea? The question must have come to generation after generation of workmen building houses, most of them for wealthy summer residents, on the other dunes in a system that stretches southwest a mile and a half to the shore of Georgica Pond. Steep sand hills flank the south side of Apaquogue Road. An almost perfect circle of dune fills most of the triangle between Darby Lane, Baiting Hollow Road, and Georgica Road. A long dog-leg ridge is just to its east. Part of this is "Major Weaver's Hill," beloved to three generations of young sledders, which was the backdrop to an amazing production some years back when Adolph Green lent his house, once Major Weaver's, for a wedding. It caught on fire as food for the reception was in preparation, but in accordance with strict Jewish custom, the wedding continued on the broad lawn as the house went up in flames atop the dune behind. Tears flowed almost as copiously as water from the volunteer firemen's hoses, and all who watched hoped that the marriage would be better than its beginning.

These dunes, now taken over by the summer colony, were the western boundary of the original East Hampton settlement, which, centered on the picture-postcard Town Pond (or its site-to-be; "a watering pond" was "diged at the Spring Eastward" in June of 1653, five years after the English arrived), ran from Hook Pond, around which the Maidstone Club golf course is wrapped today, and its Great Swamp, to the east; to the "South Sea," the Atlantic, to the south; and to the fields of the North-west Plain stretching away to the woods to the north.

If, as the geologists tell us, the sea has been rising by hundreds of feet since the last great glacier receded, and if the ever-flowing river of sand we call the beach has been rising with it and edging inland for that entire period, where did the sand for these hills (some of them soar to fifty feet above sea level) come from? For an answer, we might look again to James Truslow Adams and his *Memorials of Old Bridgehampton*, and also to the great glacial moraine to the north and west of East Hampton, whence come a good many things on Long Island, and indeed, in the entire Northeast and North Central United States.

"At East Hampton," Adams wrote, "dune formation extends one and one-half miles inland, and the hill formation of the old moraine, south, southeast, and southwest of Sag Harbor, before it became forested was covered with drifting sand, as were also the Shinnecock Hills . . . Prime, speaking of them in 1845, says that they were then 'composed almost entirely of fine sand, which is still drifted hither and thither by the winds . . . perfectly naked except extensive patches of whortle berry, bay berry and other small shrubs.' "

It would appear that the East Hampton Sand Hills were built of material blown or otherwise transported from the exposed moraine. It seems a safe guess, however, that they were not eskers, that is, "winding, narrow ridges of sand or gravel, probably deposited by a stream flowing in or under glacial ice." The ice, a looming front said to have been several hundred yards high, never reached Apaquogue Road, not by a mile or two. So these dunes are creatures of the moraine, and very old. Maybe.

And maybe not. Why should the hills of the moraine (and indeed their offspring, the inland dunes) be well wooded now,

CODFISHERMEN AT EAST HAMPTON, 1910

a century or two after having been described as bare and barren, and not have grown a thick coat of vegetation in the 11,800 years before that?

No one knows exactly what Long Island looked like when the white men arrived. In a general way, we are told that it was well wooded; Montauk (almost completely a moraine) was described by a Hollander in 1650 as "entirely covered with trees." And there were, of course, the "plaines," great open fields which the Indians had perhaps burned clear for cultivation.

White cedar, according to the late Robert Cushman Murphy's natural history of Long Island, *Fish-Shape Paumanok*, grew thick in the fresh-water swamps at the time of the settlement. Oak and hickory covered the hills, pitch pine the barrens. White pine, that easily worked favorite of house and ship builders, was apparently not as plentiful here in those times as we now imagine, although the stand at Northwest Harbor, East Hampton, bordering the salt meadow at Northwest Creek, seems to have been large. The list of the Island's native trees is long— some seventy names in all—but many, such as the holly, red maple, scarlet oak, and red cedar, apparently grew only in isolated stands. A few, like the red spruce, are no longer found on Long Island, and the paper birch, which is now quite rare, is a species of a colder climate, a relic of the centuries when the glacier's chill persisted.

A favorite tree of the South Fork which must have been as common at the arrival of the whites as it is today is the tulip, *Liriodendron Tulipifera*. It is a handsome tree with a sturdy trunk and upsweeping branches, a white flower and a gray bark with wrinkles like an elephant. A veteran of the species stands behind the East Hampton Free Library. Its crown looms dark above the surrounding elms and is visible for miles offshore; I grew up in the shade of this tree, and as a child I thought it was the biggest tree in the world, but the Long Island Horticultural Society, which keeps an eagle eye on local matters arboreal, lists it as a mere Number 23 in girth among the tulips of Long Island. At the height of a man's chest, it is thirteen feet, three inches in circumference.

The tulip stands about two hundred feet west of the largest red mulberry on Long Island, a marvelously gnarled ancient

fifteen feet, three inches around, its bifurcated trunk held together with a heavy rusted chain. It prospers in Sholam Farber's
backyard, and he has hung a plaque on it, announcing its record
status. The Horticultural Society gives as a very rough gauge of
a tree's age, short of impiously drilling out a growth-ring
chronology, a year for each inch of circumference. This would
mean that the tulip is about 160 years old, and the mulberry
180. Perhaps they were actually planted at the same time, close
by what was in the eighteenth century a Hedges family apple-
and-pear orchard, now reduced to one woodpecker-pocked pear
tree.

The Montauks and Shinnecocks went to sea in dugout canoes
—large ones, according to the historians. The canoes are said to
have been made by charring or chiseling out the trunks of large
tulip trees. The tulip behind the East Hampton Library would,
at a guess, provide a substantial length of trunk for a canoe
perhaps twenty-five to thirty feet long—whaleboat length by
coincidence, or perhaps not, for the settlers are said to have
learned their whaling from the aborigines. Although the old
belief that the whaleboat developed from the canoe is denied by
modern small-boat experts, there may be a germ of truth in it.
Whatever the case, considerable vessels could be made by the
gouging-out, filling-with-hot-water (heated stones did the trick)
and wedging-wide method employed until recently in the
Chesapeake for great sailing log canoes, some of which are still
afloat and are similar in hull conformation to a whaleboat. It is
hard, however, to imagine such a vessel big enough to carry forty
men, as tradition says some Montauk dugouts did.

The "great Cannow" over which "Waindanch Sachem of
Meantaquit," Lion Gardiner's great friend, sued one Jeremy
Vaile in 1658 must have been such a one. According to a deposition in the East Hampton Town records, Gardiner "heard" that
the canoe was coming to his island, where he had lived since

before there was an East Hampton, called for "them that were in the house to follow me and I mett my sonn and good man Vaile coming up and I asked them whie they puled not up the Canow and they said it was time enough and I called them to goe to gett it up and we all went & Could doe nothing, and then we went agen & she was full."

The canoe had filled, something that can happen to any boat left on a lee shore when the water is choppy, and had been damaged, for she was mended "by putinge 2 peeces in to the end of her." The court found for Wyandanch, and awarded him ten shillings plus court costs of one pound, one shilling. Why had not the Sachem and his men pulled up their own canoe? I suspect that the canoe had drifted over unoccupied, cast loose through carelessness or evil design.

But at this distance little is clear, save that young David Gardiner, who twenty-two years earlier had been the first European child born in Connecticut, no doubt got a parade-ground tongue-lashing from the old soldier Lion, whom the youth and the man he became could never please. We will never know the details of this dispute, which must be one of the earliest (certainly one of the few) instances in which a red man went to the white man's court, and got satisfaction.

Chapter
XI

WE ARE NOT SURE how Wyandanch's "great Cannow" came to be cast upon the shore of Lion Gardiner's island, but we do know what the white men were doing to the landscape at that time. From the early 1600s on the East Coast to the mid-1970s on the West, the new American considered the tree a more serious enemy than he ever did the old American. East Hampton's settlers made the clearing of the land, even down to the "stubbing" of roots in the public ways, a stern and pressing duty for all. Down went the trees, some for use in building or as fuel, others to be burned or piled into stump fencing. The forest—dark, home of the Indian, wolf, bear, and "lion" (yes, even on Long Island; he was probably the lynx)—had to be destroyed.

And destroyed it was. In East Hampton, the work was nearly complete only twenty-eight years after the settlement. In June 1676 the Court of Sessions ruled that "In regard to the Scarcity of good Timber in ye Bounds of This Towne of Easthampton, and the waste thereof frequently made," cutting was to be restricted to residents and licensed outsiders, and that residents were to be prohibited from selling timber outside the town. On Long Island generally, trees were so scarce by Revolutionary times that cattle were driven into the glacial kettle holes to hide them from the eyes of lookouts at the mastheads of the beef-hungry Royal Navy; the Island was close to being the vast tree-less rolling plain that the Montauk communal pasture was, well within living memory.

It was the same almost everywhere. Block Island, twelve miles east of Montauk Point, was heavily timbered when settlers arrived in 1662. By 1714, tree cutting had to be restricted. Today, and for as long as anyone can remember, Block Island has been tree-bald.

America's timber went fast, and much of it did not come back until well within living memory. First-growth virgin forest is a rarity within the bounds of what is now the United States; almost all of today's plentiful woodland, particularly in the East, is second or third growth on land once cleared for timber, pasture, or crops. There was more to the question than utility, however. To a good American, a tree, rooted and on end, was generally a nuisance, a source of leaves needing to be raked, a challenge, an opponent to be cut down to size. Questions of conservation, while they obviously occurred to the wise who asked the Court of Sessions for its ruling, were probably rarely raised, and they were never sentimental; ornamental trees were not for the frontier, which Long Island was, a section of the first frontier in North America.

It seems entirely possible that the Sand Hills at East Hampton, first mentioned in the records of the early nineteenth century, were man-created, in that man—the white man—cut the trees that anchored the sand that then blew to pile into the dunes that marched to leeward to invade the fields that he had taken from the red man. Or perhaps they weren't fields when taken, merely natural meadows, like "the Littell plaine," now the most expensive real estate in the East Hampton summer colony. This area between the Apaquogue dunes and the Atlantic was apparently open at the settlement, good natural pasturage or tillable acreage within easy distance of the infant village. Again, it may be that the Sand Hills predate the settlement and go back to early post-glacial times. These are possibilities; there is one probability—that there was no problem before man began the large-scale modification of his surroundings to suit his needs. If the dunes were there, they were probably well wooded and anchored until tree cutting began, and if they weren't anchored, no one cared; if they arose as a result of tree cutting on the moraine and inched down on East Hampton—and all bare dunes are in motion, however slow, pushed by the northwest wind—that, too, was man's doing.

This, again, is one of those problems with nature that seem to be part of our national heritage and are really problems with ourselves. The solution in 1736 was "a sufficient fence"; fences loomed large in our history until the closing of the West and the last masked rider's gallop off into fiction, wire cutters in one gloved hand. In Colonial days, fences had a practical importance, although the absence of fencing could be symbolic as well; the East End Puritans did not enclose their burying grounds, as a sign that death was not the end, that what was buried was not of any great importance. The essence, the soul, was Elsewhere, and besides, the graveyard grass grew green and tall for the stock, which roamed the highways and common lands, of which the cemeteries were a part. A fence around a burying ground smacked of Popery as much as a crucifix in church, Christmas, or May-pole dancing did; it also meant a great waste of forage.

Down along the ocean, the fields and pastures were fenced where they ended, behind the dunes, to keep the cattle from the beach banks. The settlers recognized the value of beach grass in stabilizing the dunes; in addition, once they were on the dunes, the cattle would stray down to the beach itself, where they could amble for miles in an afternoon along the sand. On the well-fenced upland, with frequent cattle gates across the highways, a stray could not roam far, so these were often rented as "let lands" for grazing and were largely turf until well into the twentieth century. Where fields met bays and ponds, labor (and, when the trees became scarce, material) could be saved by building "water-fences" extending into the water; this was not practical on the ocean side.

Beaches themselves were "passing highways," used well into this century on the great spring and fall cattle drives to and from the summer pastures at Montauk. Heirs of the East Hampton English who had bought Montauk directly from the Indians in 1660 received pasturage in proportion to their shares; farmers from villages further west paid for the privilege, and thousands of head of cattle made the drive, the eastbound herd growing as each hamlet contributed its share, and the westbound diminishing in like fashion. As a highway, the beach, at low tide in particular, was a good deal better than most roads until modern times. The sand was smooth, clean, and likely to be completely free of the flies and mosquitoes that made travel in the warm months a torture until the decline of the horse and the ascendancy of public-health notions. The drive of several days, which continued under a fee arrangement after "The Proprietors" sold Montauk in 1879, was a community enterprise and a popular entertainment, as much frolic as work.

It was especially important to cross narrow, marshy Napeague along the beach, given the inland insect population. The beach there—yellow and packed hard underfoot where it is damp from the waves' wash, soft and white higher on the beach—is sand from the glacial moraine that composes most of Montauk, an almost-island. The sand is the distillation of the huge mounds of gravel, rock, and clay pushed there by the great glacier's ice. The finer elements—the clays and soils—are dissipated as Montauk's bluffs erode; the larger stones settle to the narrow beach below, there to be finally ground down themselves into the smallest stones of all, grains of sand.

Pushed by the easterly winds of bad weather and a great westering swirl of the current in the New York Bight running counter to the Gulf Stream offshore, the lighter stones begin their own progress west along the Long Island shore. They are sorted by weight in some complex fashion; the huge boulders roll down the eroding bluff and never move again until they have been worn down; cobbles and gravels are pushed and arranged by some equation of forces that is no doubt calculable but nevertheless staggers the imagination. At Montauk proper, at the foot of the bluffs, stretches of smooth sand alternate with runs of stones; sometimes cobbles of one size will be piled in long windrows, separated from others higher or lower on the beach as neatly as if they had been sorted by some compulsive stone grocer. But just as the whole progress of the sand to the westward is a net motion, two steps forward and one back, the sorting process gradually achieves its end until the beach is pure sand without a rock in sight, except for a few quartzite pebbles in the trough where the waves break at low tide.

The process continues offshore, down that long slope to the ancient beach front miles away and fathoms deep. It does not, however, go on forever. The Army Engineers contemplate that offshore sand these days with greedy eyes, for if it were pumped and applied to the beach with care and regularity it might solve, for the geological moment at least, our erosion "problems," for which "processes" is a better and more accurate word. The Engineers have mapped the "known sand reserves" off Long Island with care. The sand, at least in mineable form, extends perhaps seven miles offshore at East Hampton, and on the diagrams it has a funnel shape, widening to the west, as might be expected, because of the prevailing drift. Offshore of the sand, nautical charts show the bottom covered with such delicacies as "gn M S Sh"—green mud, sand, and shells. This information meant a great deal to a mariner making a landfall after a crossing under sail from Europe. A cast of the tallowed dipsey (deep sea) lead; forty-two fathom, green mud, sand, shells; a whiff of white pine and maybe drying codfish; a twinge in the starboard knee joint; fifty miles s'sutheast of Ponquogue Light, b'God. That was the nature of navigation before the days of chronometers and radar.

This inexorable river of sand has moved upward and edged inland at precisely the rate of rise of the sea for the past 12,000 years, sliding sideways and leaving an ever-widening but slower-moving plume of sand offshore. At East Hampton, the visible part of the flow first touches the great fertile outwash plain. The point of contact is at Wiborg's Beach—Pink Beach, the newcomers call it. Perhaps they detect a subtle change in the sand's color as it picks up a tinge from the potato land, which was once grain fields; Long Island was one of the nation's great wheat areas before the Midwest came under the plow. It is here that outwash plain first meets beach. To the eastward, all the way to Montauk, where the moraine drops straight to the sea with no outwash plain at all, relatively stable ranges of swales and dunes separate the beach from the upland, except at Napeague, where there is no upland between bay and ocean. Railroad tracks and highway parallel each other across this low bar today, flanked for most of the four miles of sandy strip between Amagansett and Montauk by pitch and black pines, new growth which nearly conceals the high dunes to the south along the ocean beach a half mile or so away, and the lower dunes along Gardiner's Bay to the north. During major storms, bay and ocean mingle at Napeague's narrowest spot, sometimes washing out the tracks and sending salt water over the highway to make Montauk an island (again) for several hours.

Back to the westward in East Hampton Village, at Wiborg's, what the Nature Conservancy—a nonprofit landholding trust of sincere ecological bent and have-your-cake-and-eat-it-too appeal to wealthy landowners—calls the double-dunes area begins. Wiborg's is the narrow apex of a four-mile-long triangle with its base between high ground at Amagansett and the sea—a base wide enough to be occupied by subdivisions. The apex at Wiborg's is barely big enough for a small parking lot; a few hundred yards farther along it has broadened sufficiently to hold the Maidstone Club's swimming pool, cabanas, and several hundred sportive members of The Ruling Class. Between the club proper, a massive building looming on the upland bluff at the edge of its carefully tended golf course, and Amagansett, the Conservancy has been given much of the duneland. This double-dunes tract is a tangle of sand hills heaving like a confused cross-sea. The fields stretching down from the north drop abruptly to the sand, the slopes covered by wind-trimmed shad-bush, beach plum, and holly, the crest guarded by a long and wide-spaced line of understated summer homes, shielded one from another by patches of gnarled black cherry and oak. The primary dunes, facing the beach, stand untouched, a tribute to the taste and wisdom of those who built on the upland, and who then owned the dunes.

Toward Amagansett, the area between the upland and the frontal dunes is wider, and in places there is standing water, small fresh-water marshes lined with phragmites, reeds, and cat-tails, dotted with grasses and bordered in places by cranberry bogs. These, to the old timers, were The Glades, and in times long gone they were extensive enough for rowboats and canoes. Glade in this sense, as in Everglades, probably comes from an old meaning of "glad": shining. And the remaining glades still shine in the morning sun, gladly through their fringe of water grass.

Their presence holds a hint of this low area's history: from Wiborg's to Amagansett East, the double-dunes area was probably once under water. The sharp inland bluff was the beach front; as the offshore bar grew, it formed a dune line enclosing the long wedge, which became a bay and is now sand hills and fresh-water marsh. Before this happened, probably not so long ago in geologic time, the Highlands, the tumbled morainal hills east of Amagansett, were a headland, and Montauk was an island. This, however, was before historic time, before the arrival of the East End's first settler, Lion Gardiner.

GARDINER, MY GRANDMOTHER maintained, was short, red-haired, and fond of a blue coat with brass buttons. She knew this because she saw him, or what was left of him and his clothing, on her way home from school one day in 1886. Noticing some activity in East Hampton's South End burying ground (even as a child she was possessed of the relish for the macabre that made her kitten-drowner for all her old lady friends five and six decades later), she walked over to investigate. Lion's remains were being exhumed preparatory to reburial under the recumbent stone knight covered by an ornate marble canopy which can be seen today, a bit of Victorian homage. The old soldier had been below ground for more than two centuries when my grandmother saw his remains, which were probably shrunken by time, for his contemporaries called him a tall man. His coffin had long since rotted away, but she said traces of his coat remained, and some wisps of reddish hair. A Montauk Indian, a member of the Pharaoh family—a name applied by East Hampton's Old Testament Christians to the clan that provided the last "Kings" and "Queens" of the Montauks—was the gravedigger.

It would be interesting to know what passed through that Pharaoh's mind as Wyandanch's blood brother, that plain, blunt-spoken man, was moved from his pine-box grave to a new and pretentious resting place. In the inventory of Lion Gardiner's possessions compiled at his death in 1663, there is listed, in addition to such items as a bung-borer, two wedges, 11 harrow teeth, a "pt of a Corslet." Lion's effigy wears a full suit of armor, as if the reality of his life were not enough.

Lion Gardiner, who came to America in 1635 at the age of thirty-six, and to his island four years later, is perhaps a minor figure in Colonial history, but he has received less attention than he deserves. This may be perhaps because he fits into the category of neither New England history nor New York history; having played a part in both, he falls between them. He was a professional soldier, variously described in the records on his arrival in Boston as a sergeant, lieutenant, and captain. He had trained in the Low Country wars under Maurice of Nassau, Prince of Orange, who brought order, drill, and professionalism to Europe's armies and new dignity to Gardiner's branch of the art of war—military engineering. Before Maurice, engineers had been a lesser breed; Prince Maurice let them wear swords and treated them like gentlemen.

Engaged by Lord Saye and Sele and Lord Brooke of the Connecticut Company, Gardiner was brought to America to establish a fort at Saybrook, at the mouth of the Connecticut River and just across the Sound from the eastern end of Long Island. Stopping at Boston, he worked on fortifications at Breed's Hill, the actual site of the battle of Bunker Hill a hundred and forty years later. At Saybrook he fought the Pequots against his better judgment, carrying out what was at base a mercantile policy he considered short-sighted and wrong-headed. In

Connecticut the British and Dutch trading spheres were in conflict; Gardiner, whose wife was Dutch and whose military experience had been in Holland, was a natural choice as Saybrook's commander—if conciliation and common sense were expected. His advice went unheeded; war ensued with the Indians, and he fought obediently and bravely.

A new theory expounded by Dr. Lynn Ceci of Queens College explains quite logically the politics of the time and the higher policy about which Gardiner may have harbored doubts. According to Ceci, the English expansion down the coast from Massachusetts appropriated the sources of wampum along the coast and its makers, as part of a larger economic warfare against the Dutch. Wampum was apparently unknown, at least in its sophisticated cylindrical form, among the Indians until around 1600, when the introduction of European steel drills—"muxes"*— made its manufacture possible. Wampum was the coin of the beaver trade, and the inland natives were quite as mad for it as the Europeans were for beaver. The English, after occupying the source of the wampum—the Connecticut shore and later Long Island—were able to outbid the Dutch for furs.

Wyandanch, who sold the island to Lion Gardiner, had come to know him at Saybrook. Through this friendship and Wyandanch's later assumption of the leadership of the Montauks and de facto sovereignty over all the Long Island Indians, there was general peace in the area. It is possible to think of Gardiner as a Colonial administrator along the lines of those who are familiar in later chapters of the history of the British Empire, Clive of India or Brooke of Sarawak. Certainly his island was a military-economic outpost, strategically situated to control traffic

---

* One hundred muxes were part of East Hampton's purchase price in the second, backup transaction with the Montauks after a deed had been obtained from the Earl of Stirling.

in and out of Peconic Bay, the best source of whelks, which were the raw material of white wampum, on the coast, as Dr. Ceci suggests.

Gardiner's reputation among the Indians was excellent. Wyandanch thought enough of Gardiner to deed him what was to become the Town of Smithtown, prime Long Island real estate today worth hundreds of millions of dollars, and to describe Gardiner in the deed as "the most honorable of the English nation heare about us." The gift was made in 1659; not all the Indians may have approved of it, for Wyandanch died later that year, reputedly by poison.

Gardiner lived four more years, and by his death the frontier had edged somewhat west; across the Sound, King Phillip's War was to flare a decade later, and war continued with the Dutch, who gave up Nieuw Amsterdam the year after Gardiner's death. Looking back in his *Relation of the Pequot Warres*, Gardiner had observed that his rough-hewn account of past events might ruffle some; he had never been, he said, one to "endure nor abide the smoothing plane." His bluntness extended to his will, in which he counseled his wife to remember, in her provisions for their son David, that he, as a young wastrel, "hath forced me to part with a great deal of my estate to save his credit."

It could not have been easy, following in Lion Gardiner's footsteps. David's son John, an infant at Lion's death, grew up to be a great lover of squaws and rum. He was Captain William Kidd's host on his 1699 visit. Kidd, a prominent seaman of New York, had been dispatched by the Colonial authorities to the Indian Ocean in 1696 to battle the pirates then rampaging there. His activities shortly came under suspicion; it was alleged that the watchman had joined the thieves and was plundering neutral vessels under the pretext that they were carrying French passes, and were hence fair game; war between the British and French had ended with the Treaty of Ryswick in 1697 but it continued in the Indian Ocean, which was out of earshot at the time. Kidd's business arrangements with prominent New Yorkers, including the Royal Governor, Lord Bellomont, have been a subject of speculation ever since his execution at London in 1701. The belief that he was killed to spare his backers embarrassment or worse is as persistent as rumors of his great treasure still to be found.

The only treasure we are sure about was left at Gardiner's

THE FISH FACTORY AT PROMISED LAND, 1971

Island by Kidd, in the care of John Gardiner. It included gold coin, gold dust, silver, jewels, and various other valuables. After Kidd's arrest, Gardiner turned it over to the authorities and was no more suspected of complicity in the affair than were most of New York Colony's other notables, which is not to say that his innocence was regarded as proven.

Lion's grandson was jocularly known as Lord John, and it was told of him that a priest at New London in Connecticut asked about his character, after Gardiner supposedly had made tentative inquiries about converting to Catholicism. The questions were addressed to a man in John Gardiner's employ, who was vague and evasive. The priest pressed the matter: "Then his character in the main is good?"

"In the Main," came the answer, "he might pass for a good man, but on his Island he is a devilish rogue."

The relationship of the Gardiners to the townspeople of East Hampton has always been amicable enough—at arm's length. Writing to John Winthrop, Jr., later governor of Connecticut, at New London in 1650, two years after the settling of East Hampton, Lion Gardiner inquired about the possibility of hiring a pastor for the new village. It was, Lion wrote, "our determination; not to have above 12 families, and wee know that we may pay as much as 24 in other plasis, by reson that we are to be but few, we are resolvid not to resave [receive] anie, but as ar fit for Cherch estate, being rather wiling to part with sum of theas hear, then to resave more without good testimonie." One wonders which of East Hampton's revered founding families Gardiner would have been "wiling to part with," and why.

The young cleric who arrived as a result of the correspondence, Thomas James, was hired at fifty pounds a year and began a ministry which lasted until 1696, when he was buried in the South End Cemetery near Gardiner, his head resting in the opposite direction from that of the others buried there, so that he would awake on Judgment Day facing his congregation and presumably ready to preach a sermon appropriate to the event. James and Gardiner, as the leading men of the community, were excused from the arduous and smelly duty of cutting in on beached whales, either those killed by the English and Indian crews or drift whales which might have been dead for months. Instead, they were assessed a jug of rum apiece, to fuel the others.

David Gardiner's third son, Lion, was hunting deer at Three

Mile Harbor in the fall of 1723 with Samuel Bennett, whose grandfather Samuel had come to Gardiner's Island in 1639 as an employee of the first Lion. Bennett's gun discharged, and Lion fell dead. Bennett was charged with murder but was acquitted. An accident? Those who indicted Bennett must not have thought so. Whatever the case, it has never been easy to be a Lord of the Manor (a dubious title stemming from a patent granted by Royal Governor Thomas Dongan to David Gardiner in the 1680s) in a democratic society. The Bennetts are one of the largest Long Island families; their primacy of settlement matches the Gardiners and predates the oldest of old families in the East End Towns; many members are prosperous, even wealthy; others are socially vis-à-vis the Gardiners precisely where they were nearly three and a half centuries ago. One longs for a foundation to land a sociological expedition on these shores.

In the 1920s my grandmother, as curious as she had been in her childhood and still fascinated by the Gardiners, visited that family's Brown House on Main Street in East Hampton. It was about to be moved back from the sidewalk, where by special dispensation its front steps had been allowed to extend into the public right of way, to the position it occupies today, about two hundred feet away from the noise of traffic. David Johnson Gardiner of the ninth generation, an aged bachelor, showed her through the ancient structure. In the packed dirt of the cellar floor lay a tombstone, broken at the base and face up. It read, by Grandma's later recollection: "Rachel Schellinger, wife of David Gardiner, Nov. 8, 1691–Dec. 16, 1744." The stone had toppled in the South End Cemetery, and no one had bothered to restore it. "Some local woman one of my ancestors married," the modern David observed.

Chapter XIII

A HEADSTONE SOMEWHAT OLDER than Rachel Schellinger Gardiner's still stands in the Sagg Cemetery, not far from the house occupied by the man it remembers: "Coll Henry Peirson desesed November the 15 in the 50 yeare of his age 1701." Henry Pierson was a contemporary of John Gardiner, and one of the most prominent citizens of eastern Long Island in his day. He was an active man in the prime of life and a lieutenant colonel in the Provincial militia when one morning in 1699 he looked out of his window over the beach banks a quarter mile south and saw a vessel offshore. From that instant his life was changed, and it was no doubt foreshortened by the events that followed.

The vessel was the *Adventure*, a "hagboat" or "hakeboat" of the North Sea or Dutch type, displacing 350 tons, built at Ipswich in old England for the coal trade. She mounted twenty-two guns, twenty of them sakers, long-barreled naval guns throwing a six-pound ball, and two of them demi-culverins, ten-pounders a bit longer in the chase. It was an impressive battery for an ex-collier with a crew far too small to man that many guns.

The *Adventure* was described, in a notice circulated by her owners after she was missing, as "yellow painted only the Bugilugs between the Windows are black"—that is, she was trimmed with black at the stern. Her crew of twenty-five was, when Pierson saw her, headed by Joseph Bradish, "of ordinary Stature, well sett, round visage, fresh complexion, darkish hair, pock-fretten, and aged about 25." The men ranged in age from thirty-five, Andrew Martin, "Short, thick great Lips, black bushy hair, Scot," to fifteen, William Saunders, "ordinary stature, well sett, fresh coloured, black hair." It included John Westby, "Short, red hair, kept on board by force, Chyrurgeons mate," and Tee Witherly, "Short, very small, black, blind of one Eye," aged eighteen. They were, at best, mutineers, and at worst, pirates; they had seized the *Adventure* the previous September at the Island of Nias off Sumatra and picked their boatswain's mate, Bradish, as captain. Bradish and Kidd were to hang side by side "up in Gibbets a Sundrying" at Wapping Old Stairs, London, two years later.

A deposition taken by the authorities from one Simon Bonan:

The said examinant saith that upon Tuesday the 21st of this last March he was at East hampton on the Island of Nassau and did see a ship rieding at anchor off the said Town of East Hampton, upon the South Side of the Island, whereupon he the said examinant together with one Capt. Mulford, and some others belonging to the said Town, took a Whale boat and went on board the said ship wch the said Seamen said was of burthen about 370 Tuns 22 Guns and belonged to London, the Captain was ashoar but the mate was aboard, and said they came from Guinea but they saw no negros aboard, he said he was bound for Pensilvania, they sold some small armes to some of the people who went aboard with them, that she was navigated with 25 men or there abouts, they said she had sundry goods aboard, but had orders not to break bulk nor to Sell any goods, but found the people very much [illegible] and that they had been from London 15 months. Then this Examinant returned ashoar, he saw the Captain ad Jno. Mulfords house with Coll Peirson and two Ministers with him, and afterwards heard that Coll Peirson went with the said Capt. to New London, and that he had hired three Sloops, one at Southampton and two at Southold, and the next day the ship was gone I heard that she went to the Eastward, having taken a pilot called Samll. Hand along with him.

Before the *Adventure* went eastward, where she was unloaded into the sloops well offshore and where some of her guns were fired down through her hold to sink her, Bradish had left with Colonel Pierson "four baggs, two of which had as he said a Thousand Dollars or pieces of eight in each and the other two baggs had as he said four hundred Dollars or pieces of Eight in each . . . a small bagg of Jewells . . . Two small guns, and a Cask of Powdr of about 60 weight . . . one Jewell and a small bagg of peices of eight."

The jewels, in the course of proceedings under which Pierson was held to be "equally guilty with Bradish" under the "Statute 28 of Henry VIII," were pronounced by Bonan, a jeweler, to be false. This appraisal dismayed the Earl of Bellomont, the governor, who had hoped they would be worth £10,000, and may have hoped some of that sum would end up in his pocket. Disappointed or not, Bellomont obtained Pierson's royal pardon through the Council of Trade in London, assuring its members that the colonel, despite a brush with bad company, "has a fair character and is a man of substance and member of the present Assembly." In reply, the council encouraged Bellomont in his anti-piratical efforts, sympathizing with "the difficulty" of such work "in a place where they are so much favoured," that is, Long Island, known also at the time as the Island of Nassau.

Captain Mulford was Justice of the Peace Samuel Mulford,

like Pierson a friend and associate of Josiah Hobart, sheriff of Suffolk and a resident of East Hampton. Mulford's was a militia rank, although he was a noted whaleman and was to become, like Pierson, a member of the Provincial Assembly, of which the latter had been Speaker. Simon Bonan was a Jew, apparently a familiar and respected figure on the South Fork, although not a resident; he had been entrusted with the carrying of tax receipts to the authorities in New York. With Bradish at the East Hampton home of Samuel's brother John Mulford (a former justice of the peace and an incumbent East Hampton Town Trustee) were the Reverend Ebenezer White of Bridgehampton, seven years out of Harvard and four years ordained, and the Reverend Nathaniel Huntting, a year behind White at Harvard and the holder of a 1696 master's degree from that institution. He was supply minister at East Hampton and was to be ordained that fall of 1699. White, Huntting, and Bradish were in their twenties; the Mulfords and Pierson were in their late forties or fifties; Bonan's age is unknown. Taken together, that assemblage, which probably took place in what now appears to be the basement of a house at the eastern corner of Mill Hill Lane and Main Street in East Hampton (the original house had a stone-walled first floor, most unusual on eastern Long Island) was an unlikely one. The only local luminaries missing were John Gardiner, soon to receive Kidd on his island, and Sheriff Hobart.

The two young ministers had long lives ahead. Their careers ran parallel, and both ended in the New Light movement half a century later. As Harvard graduates, they were representatives of the focus of seventeenth-century American intellectual life. Both were succeeded by Yale graduates; Huntting's successor, Samuel Buell, could never boast of having dined with a pirate, but he did act during the Revolution as what the uncharitable might call a spy for the British, albeit managing to be remembered as a patriot. The Mulfords, too, had long lives ahead.

Samuel was to become known as Fishhooks Mulford, a firebrand in the Assembly. A generation later he would have been a mate to the New England revolutionaries. Pierson's short remaining life was wracked with worry until the arrival of his pardon, and Bradish, seized and imprisoned in Boston, combined an escape and an apparent romance (the girl helped him to flee jail, probably with the connivance of a relative of Bradish, who was a native of Massachusetts and had used the names of friends-in-common to impress people at East Hampton during his visit there). He was recaptured and shipped to England with Kidd to be executed.

The record is sketchy, but it is plain that Pierson helped Bradish arrange the disposal of the *Adventure*'s cargo, a manifest valued at £13,000 (Kidd's treasure was worth by his own estimate £100,000; both sums represent vastly larger amounts in today's coin). This necessitated the involvement of various worthies in Connecticut, Rhode Island, and Long Island. Samuel Hand, the pilot, for instance, was a scion of one of East Hampton's founding families. Despite his involvement with pirates, he led a long life and died in 1755 aged about ninety.

It would have been difficult, in 1699, to have gathered in any of the Colonies a more promising or a more cosmopolitan group of men than those assembled that night at John Mulford's with the pirate Bradish. Bradish's voyage back from Nias at the far end of the globe, an island almost on the equator which had been eyed by the Dutch for three decades but which was not to be pacified by them until 1857, was one of several such in that spring of 1699. A general exodus of freebooters was under way from the Indian Ocean, possibly spurred on by the belated arrival of news of peace between France and England, for stable conditions were recession-signals in the pirate trade. Bradish was elected captain of the *Adventure* because of his skill in navigation after its rightful commander, a wrathful Thomas Gulleck,

author of the "wanted" description of the vessel and its errant
crew quoted earlier. Bradish was only a month or two ahead of
Kidd in the same passage, and like Kidd, he let his crew slip
ashore, a few here, a few there. Both commanders seem to have
had a way with people in high places. In Kidd's case, prior
business connections apparently gave him hope for a safe and
prosperous return; Bradish may simply have allowed his money
to talk.

"From London in fifteen months?" Pierson, the Mulfords, the
ministers, and Bonan all knew that it was possible to take three
months to cross the Atlantic, but not fifteen months. Bradish was
said to have been headed for Gardiner's Island, which, as we
know, was one of Kidd's ports of call, but the wind did not favor
him, and the *Adventure* was scuttled off Block Island. There is
more here than meets the eye, more than we will ever know,
intrigue and complicity at high political levels perhaps. If we
knew the details, of course, there would be an end to the sort of
romantic speculation inspired by the thought of those two young
Harvard clerics listening across the table to the pirate fresh from
Sumatran waters.

Chapter XIV

ONE DAY IN THE LATE 1950s my mother and I crossed to Gardiner's Island. She hadn't been there for a decade, and one of the gamekeepers, a hunting companion of her father's, had asked us over. It was a clear day in August, and we had a pleasant sail over from the head of Three Mile Harbor, six or seven miles, in my catboat, the *Old Torrup*, christened with the local name of the snapping turtle she resembled in broad beam and stately pace. Our host took us around the island by Jeep. Toward the south end, an open plain slopes up to the crest of the bluff. Young mallards were running in the grass as we approached Everett Tuthill's fishing shanty, long abandoned and perched at the edge of the bluff.

Everett had been a friend of mine; we shared my grandfather's first name. He came down each summer in the 1940s from East Marion on the North Fork to live on Gardiner's Island, under a lease arrangement, with another man and a woman who did the cooking, an innocent *ménage à trois* among people in late middle age that amused us youngsters at the Edwards Brothers dock at

Promised Land. They came over every few days for ice and soda pop and to ship the fish lifted from Everett Tuthill's string of traps or pound nets. I was as fond of their boat, an ancient converted sloop of graceful sheer, as I was of them, and it saddened me, a decade and more later, to see their summer quarters on Gardiner's Island abandoned, with the door swinging

EVERETT TUTHILL'S CHAIR

open and a great hole in the roof. Their dock, down below, was gone except for a few broken pilings. A lump of rusty iron in shallow water was all that remained of their donkey engine; they had grown too old for fishing and had given it up at the end of a season.

We went into the shanty. "Anything here you want," our guide said, "take it. She'll all be gone over the bluff before long." The building had been built perhaps sixty years earlier a hundred feet or more from the eroding bank; now one corner jutted out into space.

There was one chair in the shack's three rooms, a heavy thing in what I thought of as firehouse style. Most people today would call it a captain's chair, and I suppose it qualified by use if nothing else. It was wobbly and wired together with threaded rods, nuts at either end, which had been in place long enough to have worn holes in the arms and seat two and three times their diameter. Its low back had been built up, apparently some years after the rest of the chair had been constructed, with two heavy pieces of wood to a height of some three inches above the arms. Turning it over, I could see on the underside of this back a series of holes, some still occupied by the stubs of spindles, showing that the chair had once had a high back in Windsor style. We threw the thing in the back of the Jeep.

The wind had picked up, and when my mother and I returned to the boat basin I knew that we would have to make the trip back to Three Mile Harbor, up to windward, under power. We put the chair in the wide cockpit of the catboat, and my mother sat in it as we pounded our way back against the northwester. It was a golden afternoon, and as she sat placidly in the old chair, spray gradually soaking the green kerchief she had tied over her head, I thought of one of her stories, about another chair, a small rocker with arms. That one, she said, had gone upstate, to Plattsburgh on the Canadian border, after the Revolution, with Phebe Miller, "you know, she married a Terbell." Poor Terbell was killed in the War of 1812, and his widow returned to East Hampton in the rocker, rocking down the Hudson for two weeks aboard a sloop, and then rocking the length of Long Island for two days aboard a farm wagon, surrounded by her five fatherless children.

My sister rocks now in Phebe Miller Terbell's chair, and I am sitting in the Gardiner's Island souvenir. It is the most comfortable perch in the house, but it has one fault. It makes its occupant want to stretch out, ankles crossed, hands clasped upon belly. In this attitude the modified back (whoever did that alteration knew his work) fits gently beneath the shoulder blades and prevents one from sliding slowly out of the chair as one inevitably falls asleep, perhaps to dream about pound nets and pirates.

Chapter XV

THE ARMY ENGINEERS' CHARTS of the offshore sand available for their Long Island anti-erosion scheme show several funnel-shaped lodes opposite the inlets through Great South Beach, known to the world at large as Fire Island. At Moriches and Shinnecock, farther east, the sand that might be available for pumping onto the erosion-narrowed strand is not there; most of it has been swept through the inlets and makes boating in the shoal-spotted, shallow Great South Bay a task worthy of one of Twain's Mississippi River pilots. Another sand-shy area is indicated on the ocean bottom just east of Amagansett, where there is no inlet.

Once there was, however. It was closed by the bar we call Napeague Beach, but the signs of the open strait that once was there are easy to see. The sand, which might be offshore but was swept into the strait or inlet, has become Napeague itself. The name means "Water Land" in Indian, but today it is more a sand land, a region of dunes and swales and sparse vegetation.

On the South Shore of Long Island, where the cumulative set

of the surf and current is generally from east to west, bars grow in that direction. Fire Island, the long stretch of sand guarding the central and western portion of Long Island from direct assault by the open sea, is extending itself to the west at a rapid rate. Fire Island Light, built alongside Fire Island Inlet, has been left some eight miles behind in a century, as the inlet hotfoots it westward toward Coney Island and New York. Thus, we would expect Napeague Beach to have grown from Montauk toward Amagansett, and so it probably did.

There is evidence, in fact, that it may still be growing, not from east to west, but from north to south. When East Hampton was settled by the whites, according to David Gardiner, author of the early-nineteenth-century *Chronicles of East Hampton* and a member of the seventh generation of his family in America (and one of a multitude of Davids in that tribe), the Napeague oceanfront dunes were lower than in his day, and the beach—the beach proper, that is, for what we call Napeague Beach may be an indication of its state within historic times—was inland of its present line. It was so much so, according to Gardiner, that the open strand was in clear view from First House—that is, the first house one came to on Montauk in the old days, one of three such headquarters for the overseers of the common pasturage there. Standing on the site of First House today, next to its small burying ground, and looking westward, one sees the backs of some of the most magnificent sand hills on the Northeast coast; the beach is beyond them and out of sight. These are new dunes; their growth and the seaward trend of the beach have been mapped in the century and a half since the first accurate surveys were made in these parts. They show Napeague to be one of the few beaches along the Atlantic shore of Long Island where there has been little or no erosion. More than that, there has been an actual net gain, at least until very recent times, and this appears to be true of the bay side of Napeague as well.

The growth of Napeague may be traced by its dune lines, some of them miles long. If there are new dunes along the ocean, there are old dunes inland, and some of them no doubt once fronted on bay or ocean. There are moving dunes, too—not that all dunes are not in motion, slight as it may be—most notably the Walking Dunes on the east side of Napeague Harbor. There are, in fact, more dunes at Napeague than one can shake a stick at, if one is in the habit of threatening sand piles. They seem to go in all directions, but some must have been relatively still in their places for many centuries, held down by beach grass, Hudsonia, poison ivy, bayberry and beach-plum roots. One dune I know alongside Cranberry Hole Road, not far from the bay, was in place sufficiently long ago for it to have been occupied by Indians—Indians of the era when quartzite pebbles were still being chipped for projectile points, before the white man's steel made better arrowheads, before the bow was discarded for the musket.

Sometimes, after a three-day northwest blow, we walk through a hollow on the side of that dune, and pick up quartz slivers and shards of clay pot. The slivers are pressure flakes, debris of the projectile-point process. Some of the shards have been incised with the edge of scallop shells in regular patterns; over a decade and more we have collected half a cigarbox full and pieced a few together with Elmer's Glue. In a hundred years, we shall have a pot.

This dune is probably one of a line that once fronted the bay, now almost two hundred yards to the north. To the northwest lies Cranberry Hole, a marsh which was a pond fit for ice cutting within living memory (it was ditched and drained to keep the mosquitoes away from the hardy pioneers of the Devon Colony, summer people arriving around 1910 from such places as Cincinnati, when eastern Long Island's popularity as a summer resort was surging). Before it was a pond, Cranberry Hole was a lagoon, cut off from Gardiner's Bay by the bar that grew into the great curve of low dune sweeping from the present Devon Yacht Club east for a mile and more. South of my Indian dune line runs another range, a higher one, extending from the tip of the glacial moraine at Amagansett—the Highlands—to the Pine Lots at Lazy Point, roughly the midpoint of Napeague's northern shore. This line, I suspect, was once the oceanfront. It runs at an angle to the present primary dune, which is roughly a half mile south.

When the English arrived, according to Gardiner's *Chronicles*, there was the skeleton of a whale well inland on Napeague, somewhere east of the Highlands. It was seen as proof of the Deluge. One spring Sunday some years back when the children were pulling each other's hair out in tufts, a desperate parent remembered Gardiner's whale and said we're going to go and find it, and cut that out or you'll be walloped. To my surprise, but not that of the children, who were young enough to hold parental infallibility as an article of faith, between the two lines of dunes on the broad flat south of Cranberry Hole Road, at the edge of a clump of twisted, stunted pines, we found on the surface three aged chunks of bone. One was a vertebra the size of my two fists together, and later the marine biologists at the American Museum of Natural History said it was from a whale. It was, however, too ancient and weathered for them to say if it was a small vertebra from a large whale, or a large vertebra from a small whale, and it went back to Amagansett to hold down papers on the living-room mantel.

The Pine Lots (allotments of land were drawn by lot; hence house lot, barn lot, cow lot, and the New Lots Avenue subway stop in Brooklyn) were deeded long ago by the East Hampton Town Trustees to private owners and occupy what is probably the top of an island of moraine between Montauk and Amagansett. Montauk stretched toward this island on the bay side in

the form of Goff Point, and at some stage this island was con-
nected to the Highlands by a growing bar, those higher dunes
which form Napeague's backbone. That the Highlands were
oceanfront bluffs (like Montauk Point, which they would re-
semble if stripped of trees and the moatlike bars and dunes which
have built up at their feet) is evidenced by their steep slopes.
From the west flank of Bendigo (reputedly Bend-I-Go: the old
bog surface is springy) Road, for instance, not far from the
Devon Yacht Club, worried owners of homes along the bluff up
at Barnes Hole (Barnes Landing, to the delicate) or indeed
owners of homes in similar situations as far west as Malibu can
take cheer. Steep slopes in glacial moraines or other unstable
hills can be anchored by vegetation. At Bendigo, of course, the
slopes have anchored themselves, but only after the lapping sea
was pushed from their bases by the formation of bars.

Out in Gardiner's Bay, deep water parallels the bluffs at
Barnes Hole and the beginning of the Highlands, a trough
pointing toward the Atlantic and what may have been the last
channel separating Montauk from the rest of Long Island. On
the east side of Napeague Harbor, another finger of deep water
points at the Atlantic. This finger is blocked in its advance by
the bar, now dune-topped, running west from Hither Hills, its
base enclosing the present state campsites below the First House
burying ground. Along this channel facing Napeague Harbor
were the predecessors of the last Long Island "fish factory" at
Promised Land. These early "pot-works" were established in the
mid-nineteenth century for the rendering of oil and meal from
menhaden, the small herringlike fish taken in seines by Oliver
Osborn and his farming relatives at Wainscott for fertilizer. The
early factories stood at the edge of what is now Hither Hills
State Park, not far from the Walking Dunes. The deep water
allowed the fishing steamers easy access to the factories, which
in the menhaden boom years had their counterparts up and down

the coast from Rhode Island to Louisiana. The channel also offered a sheltered approach to the 700-foot iron pier that for a brief period in the 1880s projected from Napeague Beach into the ocean just to the south. From the pier, nets were hung; the edible varieties of fish, in contrast to the oily, bony menhaden, or bunker, were shipped from Napeague Harbor, with a narrow-gauge railroad connecting pier and harbor. Nature, in the form of winter storms, shortly showed she abhors iron piers, and not a trace remains today. Nor is there a trace of another fishing scheme of that piscatorially speculative period, the holding pond for striped bass dug behind the beach banks by Amagansett seiners at the west end of Napeague.

The menhaden-rendering plants ran on steam and needed reliable supplies of fresh water. At Promised Land, after decades of digging shallow wells into the fresh water under Napeague and sustaining repeated damage to boilers from salt-water intrusion, generally from below the fresh water, the management of the last plant in the mid-1960s sank a deep well at the foot of the Highlands, a mile and a half away, and got plentiful good water from the underlying moraine, which contains Long Island's primary supply. A pipeline was laid to the factory just in time for its closing; centralization had entered the menhaden fishery—which hardly anyone away from the East and Gulf Coasts has ever heard of, yet which is one of the most important segments of the nation's fishing industry—and operations shifted to New Jersey.

Years before, the proprietors of the fish factory on Hicks Island, off Lazy Point, where the water situation was even more desperate than at Promised Land, had established a pumping station at Fresh Pond, Montauk, two miles to the east. Nothing is left of that operation except a concrete floor and some clinkers and fragments of boiler tubing in the oak woods alongside the pond, and a length of water main at Skunk's Hole where the

FISH-HAWK NEST AT NAPEAGUE, 1930s

main ran across the beach and out under Napeague Harbor to Hicks Island. Skunk's Hole was probably named for the aroma of the nearby factories, a stench strong enough to tarnish silver coins in the pockets of their employees.

This Fresh Pond, the one at the end of the Hicks Island main, is not to be confused with the one at Amagansett. That Fresh Pond, illogically, is salt or at least brackish water. Both were formed by the march of the sand, at Amagansett south from the Barnes Hole bluffs and at Montauk west from the bluffs north of Hither Wood and then left-facing south from Goff Point—the Walking Dunes.

The dunes walk still, but slowly, to the southeast, gradually gobbling up whole living oaks and pines and spitting them out behind as dried dead stumps, perhaps centuries later. The hill looming high over the railroad tracks just before the entrance to Hither Hills State Park is in the front rank of the Walking Dunes, and as the trackmen keep shoveling away at its feet (they have to shovel; the trains, however infrequent, unpredictable and improbable, must go through), the steeper the hill gets. Someday no doubt the dune will topple forward—tripped, as it were—and the tracks will have to be moved. Behind this great dune, which has climbed up and over the west end of the Montauk portion of the Ronkonkoma moraine, a lump known to our ancestors and the Indians, who had a fort nearby, as Nominicks, is a swamp leading to Fresh Pond. There is another, smaller swamp on the harbor side of the Walking Dunes. It was here, most likely, that the Indians had the fort. They went, like hunted rabbits, to tangles and briar patches in time of trouble. Before the Walking Dunes moved across this landscape, the two swamps were one, and not long ago, naturalists report, bald eagles nested in the Fresh Pond half of the swamp.

I've never seen an eagle there, but I have at the other end of Napeague, three miles west. An adolescent bald eagle sat brooding

on a telephone wire crossing Cranberry Hole Road just below
the Highlands one summer afternoon in 1974. Several drivers
stopped to watch, and the eagle flew off, to land in the dunes a
hundred feet away. Approached, he flapped off slowly to a tall
pine, where he spent the rest of the daylight sulking while angry
kingbirds chattered just out of reach.

The eagle was not king at Napeague, however, during the
heyday of the fish hawk, or osprey, a reign that was ended
only a decade and a half ago by DDT, that chemical giant-killer.
Until well after World War II, big fish-hawk nests, sometimes
six or seven feet across and three feet high, made of branches,
bits of rubber boot, fishline, broken toys, and bones, stood on the
dry Napeague flats, in trees or on the telephone poles.

Ma Bell's linemen, in desperation, erected substitute poles
without wires off to the side and shooed the ospreys onto them.
The ground nests (traces of a few are still visible) were a rarity
on Long Island, although they were usual enough in such isolated environments as Gardiner's Island or its southerly extension,
Cartwright Shoal. In the early 1960s a marked decline in the
fish-hawk population took place, and the East Hampton Town
Fathers (there were no Mothers until early in the next decade)
were persuaded that it was the result of a housing shortage. Town
workmen were set to building platforms, which were erected on
poles in likely spots. None, to my knowledge, was ever put to
use by an osprey, although I once saw a snow owl brooding away
a winter afternoon on one of them.

It was about then that the effect of DDT on the fish hawks
(primarily through a great reduction in the strength of the
shells of their eggs) became known. Today the only active osprey
nest on Napeague is on one of a tall pair of ITT radio towers at
Napeague's midpoint. The best nest site of all, at the top of the
tall brick chimney of the abandoned Devon Colony power plant,

has not been occupied since the early 1970s. Some say the birds will return now that DDT has been banned.

Perhaps they will, but they cannot bring back with them my childhood, when none of us knew how to pronounce the word "osprey," or bring back my grandfather, who always blew the horn of his Dodge coupé when a fish hawk passed overhead bearing a fish or an eel. Perhaps once in ten times the startled bird would drop its catch. Then Grandpa would laugh, stop the car and get out to examine whatever had fallen to earth with a commercial fisherman's eye. Sometimes the fish was worth keeping; more often it was left for the irate fish hawk, circling in outrage above, to retrieve.

Fish hawks were an object of our annual July voyage to Cartwright Shoal in the White Seineboat. Its battery was always dead, and I learned about keeping "Hands in the boat!" as we bobbed impatiently in the Promised Land basin waiting for a fresh battery. Great-aunt Minnie and Grandma and the other old ladies collected fish-hawk and gull eggs, which, they assured us, had to be infertile or spoiled to be unhatched this late in the season, to be blown and placed with a hundred others in the glass-fronted cabinet in the dining room of the Huntting house on Main Street. The birds may return, but that generation, and the eggs, and the cabinet, have disappeared, and the homestead was sold out of the family after the death of Uncle Dan, he of the belated and unsuccessful marriage.

Chapter
XVI

A MAN OF MY FATHER'S GENERATION once told me a story about fishing, and about my grandfather. The narrator had gone bunker fishing back in the 1920s, but he used the present tense; the memory was vivid, and he still did not know what to make of it. The bunker boat is hove-to off East Hampton, the only sounds the gentle hiss of steam venting from her tall stack and the creak of gear as she heaves slowly to the gentle swell. It is early July, the Fourth, and two dozen men, most of her crew, are sitting in the shade of the deckhouse out of the afternoon sun, shifting as she slowly changes her heading. The beach, a little more than half a mile away, shows white. To the west, the left, is a ragged row of summer cottages on the crest of the beach banks. To the right is the Maidstone Club. An airplane, not an unusual sight a decade or so after the Great War, chatters the length of the beach, circles the clubhouse, and lands in a field next to it.

Directly inshore is the Pavilion, the bulk of its large public bathhouse gray-shingled against the green of the trees behind. A few automobiles are to be seen parked at the foot of Ocean Avenue, alongside the Pavilion, and bathers are visible jumping in the gentle surf, black specks in their swimming costumes. Once in a while a gleeful shout carries across the water.

One of the fishermen rises, goes to the open hold and stretches down and in, coming up with a small menhaden, one of perhaps a hundred thousand caught in two sets of the long purse seine earlier in the day. Since then, there has been nothin' doin', no sign of fish; for lack of anything better to do, and because the bunkers are as likely to make their sign here as anywhere else, the fishermen are waiting for dusk and the East Hampton fireworks display. They work on shares or lays and would not think of not working on the Fourth of July, but if there is to be a free treat they might as well enjoy it.

The one active fisherman comes out of the hoister house with a short length of board. With the quick fingers of a lifetime's work with twine he lashes the bunker tail-and-gills to the board. He steps to the side and swings over, feet on the heavy protruding rubbing strake, and hanging on with his left hand as he squats and carefully places the board, fish-side up, on the water. It drifts slowly from the side of the steamer.

One of the terns which have been circling aimlessly sights the fish and cries. It hovers at thirty feet and dives, striking the fish and the board with a splash and a thump. It flops on the surface feebly, and finally shakes itself and flies off. The board drifts, and another tern dives and is stunned.

The captain, who has been watching impassively from the walkway around the pilothouse, one booted foot on the lower pipe of the railing, stands straight. "All right, boys; we'll make a set."

"Where?" someone says, looking around for a sign of fish, a

reddish glow or the feathery ripples of a finning mass of menhaden.

"Right over there."

The two heavy seine boats are lowered, half the massive damp twine in each, and the crew, all complaining at a mutter, rows off to seaward two hundred yards. The boats part and set a quarter mile of twine in a great circle, the crewmen pursing the heavy netting at its lower side with the quarter-ton tom weight of lead riding against its rings, and heave in slowly to make the circle small. A few bluefish splash in the center when the pursed seine is reduced to a diameter of a dozen feet, and are scooped out. There are no bunkers; nobody thought there would be. The seine is looped around the stern of the steamer, and the boats are hoisted, one on each quarter. As the sun sets, the first rocket of the Fourth of July display goes up and bursts white against the orange of the western sky.

A quarter century later, Captain E. J. Edwards' executors will open the office safe in his house inland across golf course and potato fields from the Maidstone Club, a mile away but a culture distant. It was a big house, a solid house, but he liked to say it had been built of fish scales, and indeed its shingles were regularly anointed with bunker oil to lengthen their life. Within the big safe, among the unpaid promissory notes, ancient deeds, and a packet of Imperial Russian railway bonds, was one of a pair of men's patent-leather dancing pumps.

Someone remembered that it had been found in the garage one night in the 1920s, when there had been a crash and the best Dodge, the going-to-church car, not the drive-to-the-dock car, had been backed out through a closed door and driven off at speed. It was found later in a hedge, moderately damaged. It was Fourth of July, and there was a big party at the Maidstone. The shoe had the name of its owner, son of a club member, inked within; it had rested in the safe, a cartridge for firing in some social or business dispute if needed, all through the Crash, the Depression, and World War II while its owner never asked about or admitted to what Captain E. J. called that "Dido with the Dodge." The shoe was put to rest shortly after the captain, and its owner has since followed both.

Chapter
XVII

THE NAPEAGUE OSPREYS Grandpa plagued with the auto horn were fond of fishing in Pond of Pines, a small tidal pool off Napeague Harbor, just south of Lazy Point Road. Pond of Pines runs to the harbor through a channel meandering between banks overgrown with salt-meadow hay and spike grass. On the banks hang mussels; in the channel's shoals hide razor clams, hard clams, and steamer clams. In the mud of the pond proper are blue-claw crabs; in its eelgrass lurk scallops and small minnows, killies. The diamond-backed terrapin has been seen at Pond of Pines, and egrets, night herons, and great blue herons feed regularly in its shallows. The hundreds of acres of salt marsh running off to the east, south, and west are the year-round hunting grounds of various hawks, and the dunes to the north—Trustee land, comprising a large part of what little is left unallotted of East Hampton Town's seventy square miles—are tracked by black snakes, and now and again a red fox. Toward the bay there is a small village of fishing shanties and summer camps, each on its small lot leased from the Trustees. Quaint, say the few tourists who ever find this out-of-the-way hamlet; an anachronism and in violation of health and building codes, say the planners; a nuisance, say the Trustees; leave us alone, say the Lazy Pointers.

Napeague, with its deerfeed flats, cranberry bogs, beach plums, pine copses, and blueberry, grape, and shadbush tangles, is good deer country. I stood behind the bay dune one winter day and watched a buck swim slowly over to Napeague from Gardiner's Island. He disappeared below my line of sight, and I waited a few minutes before walking down to the beach. On the sand a few hundred yards east were his tracks, going straight up and over the low beach bank. I walked up the bank quietly, and as my head came level with its top, the buck leaped from the bayberry ten yards away and wearily crashed off inland, wheezing great ruminant oaths.

There are raccoons on Napeague, too, and its pheasants, Asian imports and green-bandanna-ed Johnny-come-latelies to the American landscape though they may be, are fine eating indeed after their diet of cranberry and bayberry. The rabbits stick to the low spots, which ring in April and May to the song of the peeper frog, but there are voles and mice almost everywhere. The mice like Lucky Strikes. When I still smoked and we were living on Cranberry Hole Road, along the north shore of Napeague's low sandy isthmus between Montauk and the rest of Long Island, they would not walk a mile for a Camel, but they would climb up on the bedside bookcase and silently chew the ends off three or four Luckies in an open pack.

The early maps show much of Napeague as marsh, and indeed the salt meadows were valued by the settlers for winter grazing in the days before cultivated barn fodder was common. With the passing of time the meadows diminished as the land grew drier, farming practice changed, and the "medder hay" became less used, although an abandoned horse-drawn hay rake rusted on the marsh near Lazy Point until a few years ago. The Napeague meadows reverted to the marsh wrens and clapper rails, and in the late 1800s the Town Trustees began to give quit-claim deeds to portions of those areas of Napeague held by them as commonage. Beach frontage on the bay or harbor side was deeded away or leased for occupancy by fish-rendering plants.

A good deal of vacant land at Napeague—dunes and meadow running from bay to ocean—was eventually purchased by Gilbert P. Smith, the late and astute owner of the Smith Meal Company factory at Promised Land, a locality on the bay side of Napeague which may have been named by the rustic humorist who gave Egypt Lane in East Hampton Village its title. "Down Egypt" was Biblically dark and swampy; Promised Land smelled to high heaven and was the destination of bands of seasonal pilgrims, itinerant laborers looking for work, foreigners to boot. Mr. Smith confided in few people (although he once told my mother, in the course of a particularly arduous passage on the Long Island Rail Road's Cannonball from New York to East Hampton, that he had got his start in the fish-meal business by buying up his bankrupt father's small pot works on Great South Bay near Patchogue when he was twelve or thirteen; he had, he said, convinced the bankers of his sagacity and energy, apparently in contrast to those qualities in *pater familias*) but his reasons for his purchases were twofold. If he owned the land, there would be nobody living to leeward to complain about the smell of his factory, and the land was a good buy, particularly for the man who controlled the smell that kept the price down. Employing the same reasoning, he bought a good deal of Fire Island years ago, for which his heirs must thank him three times a day.

Most of the Smith purchase at Napeague is still open land, some 1,350 acres with almost three miles of oceanfront, and it will remain open. It is now a state park; the alternative was sub-division, although this would have been technically difficult until the twin problems of water supply and sewage disposal in such a low-lying area were solved, and practically difficult given the new environmentalist sentiment, which slowed the developers until the state, reinforced at a vital moment in the negotiations by the Nature Conservancy, could act.

Development would have done great harm to Napeague, of course, for if Long Island's East End landscape is delicate, this is the most delicate part of all. One motorcycle joyride across its Hudsonia and reindeer moss will leave a scar for years; its flora runs to the small and easily destroyed. There are tiny orchids in the wet spots on Napeague, and curly-grass ferns, and many varieties of mushrooms, some of which prefer the dry flats. Knowledgeable Long Islanders of East or South European extraction come each fall to pick the edible fungi, carefully cutting them from their stems with sharp jackknives to encourage next year's crop.

Untutored visitors sometimes gather whole baskets of the red-orange fruit of the bearberry, thinking it to be cranberry. But however long they are cooked, these bitter buckshot-sized berries remain inedible. The novice should know that the cranberry needs water, or at least moist ground; the bearberry grows where it is dry. If your knees get muddy picking, you are on to the real article, the cranberry.

One of the best cranberry bogs on Napeague (on, as "on Montauk," or on an island, rather than "at" or "in") runs straight as a die down the center of the isthmus. It occupies the old East Hampton Town right of way, never paved but used before its parallel state road—Route 27—was extended past Amagansett during the highway-building boom of the 1920s. Some years ago a Town highway superintendent, intent on driving the few conservationists then loose upon the landscape up the nearest tree, or perhaps merely intent on keeping his crew (all political patronage then) busy during a slack period, had the right of way bulldozed. The Caterpillar tractor's blade cut through the sand to ground water, and a marvelous bog, thirty feet wide and a mile or more long, was created. Upon reflection, it seems to me that Superintendent Roy Lester may have known exactly what he was doing—building the perfect public cranberry bog.

No matter. The bog is there, just north of the railroad tracks, over which a train sways now and again to and from Montauk, at speeds and over terrain reminiscent of the guerrilla scenes in the film version of Lawrence's adventures in Arabia. Indeed, Westerns were made along these tracks, back in the days before the moviemakers abandoned Long Island City for Hollywood, and Valentino played "The Sheik" among the dunes of Napeague in the late summer of 1922.

East of the ITT radio towers—from them are transmitted Morse messages to ships at sea: "Come home, all is forgiven"; "Disregard my 1121 Zulu. Proceed Persian Gulf"; one of the towers, a replacement after the 1954 hurricane, used to stand at Pearl Harbor, where it witnessed the events of December 7, 1941—a spur was built from the railroad tracks south across the highway during World War II. One day a sixteen-inch railway gun rolled down it to a position behind the dunes. I do not know if this behemoth was ever fired. If it was, I doubt if any record exists, at least locally. The similar weapons at Fort Hero near Montauk Point were fired several times in wartime drills, and the event lives in Montauk memory. The concussion rattled windows many miles away. The big guns might have been used but were not, for the Navy had the situation well in hand on the last day of the war in Europe, when an apparently lunatic U-boat captain torpedoed a large coal barge between Block Island and Watch Hill, Rhode Island, more or less behind the battery at Montauk but within range. He died for his sins and his fanaticism, as did all his crew, beneath an hours-long barrage of depth charges.

Such matters, while generally discussed despite warnings about Loose Lips, were not to be written about then. Nor was another feature of eastern Long Island life during the early 1940s—the parade of five-cubic-yard Colonial Sand and Gravel trucks that rumbled, day and night, trunk to tail like the elephants of Hannibal's army, toward Fort Hero. They came heavily laden from some quarry far to the west, thundering past every two or three minutes. Through East Hampton and Amagansett they roared, the pounding of their wheels cracking chimneys and gradually crumbling the yellowish concrete with which Route 27 was surfaced in those days. Across Napeague Beach they trundled, bearing sand like coals to Newcastle over a landscape all sand to another landscape equally sandy, sand to be made into concrete and poured into hollows dug in the sand of Montauk Point, concrete for great-gun emplacements.

No doubt the specifications were drawn in such a way as to exclude the lesser sands of Montauk and Napeague. We wondered, and we gossiped, but when the war was finally over and such questions could be raised in print, people were too tired, or too pleased that the war had ended, to bother. The big guns were cut up with acetylene torches, the sole victim of their deadliness an unfortunate workman who sliced with his torch into a portion of recoil mechanism still under pressure, but the tunneled concrete emplacements remain. The last I knew they were Montauk's official fallout shelters, stocked with dry biscuits and canned water against Armageddon.

The Napeague Beach sand which was not good enough for the Army is quartz sand, flecked with tiny pebbles of tan or gray feldspar, red garnet grains, and streaks of iron sand—magnetite. Our children, when younger, liked to drag a dime-store magnet on a string through the purplish deposits of the iron sand; it was mined for compasses and electrical implements from such layers, long ago, on Fire Island. Magnetite's sorting mechanism is built in; it will gladden a racist's heart and stick with its own kind. But the gradual arranging process by weight or by composition so often seen on open beaches is at work in all parts of Napeague, from the long row of cobbles like a Roman road running straight north across the broad meadow near the Walking Dunes (almost paralleling the ancient west boundary of Montauk, marked at its original north end, now far in from the living, moving beach, by a granite post, a favorite perch of hawks and owls hunting the meadow) to the layers showing against the steep side of a slid-away dune.

As a rule the finer sands or gravels are the easiest going underfoot because they pack the hardest. There are exceptions; the finest grains of sand are the best travelers with the wind, and where they are fresh-dropped by a sudden decrease in wind velocity, as on the lee side of a dune, they are loose and fluffy, a trap for the beach-buggy driver. There are puzzles in this sorting, too. Why, for instance, is the ocean beach almost always softer underfoot in one stretch a mile or so east of Amagansett than elsewhere? There are sometimes new gears in the sorting mechanism. Along the bay the apparatus was modified by the introduction of codium ("Sputnik weed"—the baymen damned it as a Communist menace when it arrived in the year of the first Russian satellite, 1957), a green and woolly seaweed which anchors itself on rocks and chowder clams, and often drags these anchors ashore in a blow. By this means, many tons of stones, each weighing a pound or two, may be placed on a few hundred yards of beach in a single northwest storm, and knowing beach walkers may collect a mess of clams without wetting a toe.

Sand and stones and movement: Napeague Beach. Below it all, of course, is bedrock, here 1,600 feet down, sloping out under the sea. The bedrock was there before the glacier, it was there before the moraine, it was there when the sea was 430 feet lower, and Montauk and the Highlands were but two pimples on the earth's surface, and not very prominent pimples at that, and Manhattan was a rocky part of the east bank well up the river to be called the Hudson. The bedrock was there thousands of years later, when the sea had risen but before the bar had emerged from the sea to join Nominicks and the Highlands and form Napeague. It will be there when the sea has risen still farther and submerged New York, New Orleans, and Los Angeles, and made Montauk an island again. Or will the sea continue to rise? Some think a new Ice Age is on its way; the world's average temperatures have been dropping since 1940, and if we are re-entering the Pleistocene, as winters of the late 1970s hint, the ocean's foot-a-century rise should shortly reverse itself, as more of the world's water is locked again in the ice cap. Until the sea begins to recede, however, we must expect the crucial factor of Long Island oceanfront life to be the sand supply. And that, unless the Army Engineers are allowed to embark upon their gargantuan offshore-dredging scheme, means we must look to Montauk, at the far end of Napeague Beach.

Chapter

XVIII

Montauk turned the young Walt Whitman positively boyish. In his *Letters from a Traveling Bachelor* of 1849, he reported on a visit: "We rambled up the hills to the top of the highest—we ran races down—we scampered along the shore, jumping from rock to rock—we declaimed all the violent appeals and defiances we could remember, commencing with 'Celestial states, immortal powers, give ear!' "

The peninsula remains, in large part, the up-hill-and-down-dale landscape that so animated Whitman, and a survivor of the general taming that has transformed a large part of America. Long Island, like most of the nation, once had many more ponds, streams, and fresh-water marshes than it does today. Montauk remains much as it was, and when Whitman and his companions reached the bottoms of those hills they no doubt found themselves panting in bogs.

On Long Island generally, as elsewhere, deforestation and drainage schemes have accelerated the runoff of rain and melted snow, the island's only source of water outside New York City's limits despite old wives' tales of underground veins stretching down from Connecticut. One ancient watercourse runs southwest through East Hampton Village, crossing a number of what we called backyards and are now lawns, to disappear a half mile later under Main Street into a storm sewer. When Guild Hall, East Hampton's galleries-and-theater community center, was built in this swale, the graybeards said the building would eventually float away, and so it almost did on February 17, 1936, the night my brother was born. For more than a decade after, the high-water mark could be seen on the circus-stripe wallpaper in the Hall's John Drew Theater; the flood would have reached well above the conductor's head, had one been in the orchestra pit that stormy night.

In later winters, when a quick thaw and rainstorm followed a long freeze, there would be water enough at the rear of a friend's house for us youngsters to voyage in a rowboat, paddling sometimes past the outhouse, rising from the waters like a lighthouse and intended for the help in an ancient office building nearby. This intermittent stream, part of the Hook Pond watershed, seems today to have been tamed, as similar watercourses have been almost everywhere on Long Island, and in almost all urban and suburban areas of the United States.

Montauk's exception rests on several factors. One reason is historic; there was little settlement at Montauk until the mid-1920s, and before that, only minor attempts at drainage, as at Ditch Plain. Another reason is the physical composition of this almost-island. Montauk's soils are finer than those in the moraine farther west and include water-impervious clays between layers of hard-pan gravel. In addition, the topography of Montauk is a jumble of hills, unconnected hollows, and kettle holes, rougher than most of the other portions of the moraine now and apparently always. The last glacial hill at Amagansett, west across Napeague Beach, the Highlands, is, however, almost as irregular as Montauk in its surface.

By its nature, such terrain holds pockets of surface water, to the degree that some areas of Montauk appear from an airplane, particularly when the many small ponds and bogs are frozen, like a shell-pitted battlefield. Yet Montauk has its natural drainage systems and its flowing brooks. One, Ogden's Run, south of Oyster Pond and not far from Montauk Point, tumbles steeply down a slope over glacial boulders. Its twists, turns, and pools are reminiscent of a mountain stream, and the stones in its bed look for all the world like the exposed bedrock of a Vermont brook. This stream flows from an upland marsh filled with lily pads and ringed with mallow, a place of frogs and dragonflies on a summer's day. Ogden's Run feeds brackish Oyster Pond its fresh-water ration; the salt comes in during northeast storms from Block Island Sound as a low sandy gut is breached. Oyster Pond was a famous place for gunning once, with the shanties of the Indian Field and Amagansett Gun Clubs in hollows back from its shores, small shingled camps redolent of roast goose and un-jugged rye. Today the pond is part of a state park, and sheldrake, broadbill, and black duck, safe from hunters, settle quickly after being put up by passing Jeeps or dude-ranch horses.

Those who judge Montauk by its mildly raucous resort-town business district, its motels, or its bustling fishing docks never realize how much of this 10,000-acre peninsula remains in a state of nature. It does so through a series of circumstances; an over-simplified list would include the fact that the Montauk Indians retained all title to Montauk for a dozen years after the settle-ment of the rest of East Hampton Town by the English; that the Indians then deeded a major interest in Montauk not to the town but to certain individuals living in it; that these whites, and their descendants, held the land as a corporation until 1879; that it was then sold by court order as a parcel to a wealthy speculator, Arthur Benson, whose family retained great portions of the land until the 1960s; and that the railroad did not reach Montauk until 1895 (to terminate precisely on top of the Montauk Indians' best cranberry bog), and good roads not until three decades later. Montauk was, then, until a scant two generations ago, a frontier remnant, largely isolated and hard to live on.

Fronting the Atlantic, Montauk begins at the west boundary of what is now Hither Hills State Park with broad sand beaches. These beaches continue, at the foot of low bluffs, to a point east of Fort Pond, a fresh-water lake nearly sundering the peninsula, and the business district, which was planted in an inappropriate spot in 1926 by Carl Fisher, founder of the Indianapolis Raceway and high-powered promoter. Montauk was to be his "Miami Beach of the North." Fisher learned some expensive lessons in city planning during the Florida hurricane later that year; Montauk businessmen paid for his mistake again in another twelve years, during the 1938 hurricane. The bluffs resume east of the low-lying business district, the beach gradually growing rockier, with sandy intervals as at Ditch Plain, toward the Point, where it is cobbled with stones ranging from baseball to house size. North of the Montauk Lighthouse, the beach gradually becomes sandier all the way to the Lake Montauk entrance channel and resumes again west of it. Periodic dredging of the channel supplies sand for the beach east and west of the stone jetties protecting the entrance, which interfere with the natural flow of sand, just as the groins along the ocean in the Hamptons do. Further west toward Fort Pond Bay, bluffs rise and the beach below is almost solid stone and coarse gravel. This continues past the Bay, Rod's Valley, Rocky Point, and Quincetree Landing, to Water Fence, the west boundary of the Proprietors of Montauk, the corporate owners under the ancient arrangement. Here, where their holdings ended, all through the three centuries when the East End villages sent their herds out for summer grazing, a split-rail barricade extended into Napeague Bay east of Goff Point and kept the cattle "on" Montauk.

"To a mineralogist," Whitman enthused, Montauk's beaches "must be a perpetual feast. Even to my unscientific eyes there

THE LEWIS KING STRANDED AT MONTAUK, 1888

were innumerable wonders and beauties all along the shore, and the edges of the cliffs. There earths of all colors, and stones of every conceivable shape, hue, and density, with shells, large boulders of a pure white substance, and layers of those smooth round pebbles called 'milk-stones' by the country children. There were some of them tinged with pale green, blue, or yellow—some streaked with various colors—and so on."

Whitman's wonder-bordered peninsula may be divided into three zones for discussion, as it sometimes is by storm tides. The first portion, four miles long and two wide, from Hither Hills and Nominicks, the first elevation at the east end of Napeague Beach, to Fort Pond, is glacial, but not as rough or kettle-dotted as the sections of the moraine farther east. It has soil fertile enough for a dense hardwood forest, much of it within the state park grounds, and contains a large fresh-water pond, Fresh Pond MunTAWK to the old-timers, to differentiate it from the Fresh Pond at Amagansett. They pronounced Montauk with the stress on the second syllable, probably in Indian fashion, and snickered in the 1920s when romantics on the Long Island State Park Commission started calling Fresh Pond "Hidden Lake." They were less amused when Robert Moses' parks employees bulldozed and burned their gunning camps near Goff Point in advance of a stated deadline for the removal of the buildings and the hunting and fishing gear within.

Much of the rolling land around Fresh Pond is more densely forested today than it has been in almost three centuries. This is in part the result of the decline of agriculture and the reversion of open land to woods, and it is in part thanks to lessened wood chopping for timber and fuel in this century, although wood-cutting, even within the state parks, has undergone a revival since the energy crisis.

Another stimulus to forest growth was the relative infrequency of major storms in the 1960s and early 1970s. This contributed particularly to such growth as that of the pitch pines on Napeague Beach during this long stretch without salt-water inundation; it is also noticeable in Hither Wood. But one factor is often overlooked. Fire, like ice, is a major shaper of the Long

Island landscape. Since the Long Island Rail Road's last steam locomotives were sidetracked in favor of diesels in the 1950s, the frequency of forest fires in Hither Wood and everywhere else along the LIRR right of way has dramatically decreased. This has been accompanied by a change in public attitude toward the ancient rural practice of burning fields and even woodland in the spring as an encouragement to new growth. The federal "Smokey Bear" campaign, state regulations on open burning, and wildlife considerations have combined to discourage the spring fires of careless or deliberate origin which were for centuries a familiar feature of country life here and elsewhere. Not everyone agrees that the deliberate fires were on balance harmful; some, indeed, argue that they kept down the ticks, encouraged the grass, and made for open, parklike woodland.

There was fire in these woods before man arrived, for lightning has always been with us; one theory holds that life itself may have begun with a lightning-sparked chemical reaction. There will be fire at the end, too, unless it comes as ice, as did Long Island's beginning, or what we see as the beginning.

At the east end of Hither Wood is Shepherd's Neck, where the communal shepherd lived in a hut behind Second House. This was literally the second house one came to. First House was four miles back, near Nominicks; Third House was four miles farther along, beyond Great Pond. The three were occupied by the families that oversaw the grazing of sheep and cattle for the Proprietors of Montauk, landlords who provided, by fee or stockholder privilege, for the summer pasturage of the eastern Long Island flocks and herds.

Shepherd's Neck stretches into Fort Pond, which is separated from salt water at the north as it is at the south by a low sandy bar. The oceanfront bar grew out from the bluffs to the east, and it is still supplied with sand from them. The bar fronting Block Island Sound and Fort Pond Bay to the north is supplied by the bluffs both east and west. It was occupied by the picturesque Montauk fishing village before the twin devastations of the 1938 hurricane and Navy construction during World War II wiped out the small houses and stores, most of them sheathed in fish-box lumber and built to multiples of this measure long before most architects had heard the word "module." Now the bar holds the New York Ocean Science Laboratory, the Long Island Rail Road's easterly station, and a few houses and businesses spared by war and hurricane. The southerly bar, between pond and ocean, contains Route 27, Kirk Park, Second House, now a museum, and Fisher's business district. Either sandbar is a place for earnest reflection in hurricane season.

The middle portion of Montauk, roughly a mile and a half east-west and three miles north-south, begins at the east bank of Fort Pond, a bank which quickly slopes into bluff and becomes Fort Hill, the eminence south of the hulk of Fisher's Montauk Manor, a vast Miami Beach–Tudor hotel brooding on Signal Hill. This portion of Montauk is generally high ground, with one great low swamp occupying the bottom of the North Neck Kettle Hole. Most of the upland was pasture and open until fairly recent times, although it has rapidly grown over with trees and brush since grazing ended. Here, in sandy places on southerly slopes, are the flat cacti which so surprise travelers yet are native to Long Island.

The real cowboys among the young Yale men in Teddy Roosevelt's regiment of Volunteer Cavalry, the Rough Riders, must have felt at home when they camped on the bare, dusty hills after their return from Cuba in 1898. As mentioned before, many of them died at Montauk, lingering victims of tropical disease and tinned provisions, a scandal of the time, and some rest here still in unmarked graves near the Manor. So do nobody knows how many generations of Montauks, the earlier bones stained with red ochre, which long outlasted the flesh it was once smeared upon in funeral ritual, and some of their graves are marked: circles of stones near the Montauk Downs golf course, once the Golf & Racquet Club.

There are better names than either of these at Montauk. The hills: Fort, Telegraph, Signal, Clapboard, and Turtle. The ponds: Big and Little Reed, Fort, Money, Oyster. The points: Burying Place, King's, Shagwong, Culloden, Cottage, Rocky, False, Montauk itself. The coves: Turtle, Dead Man's, Great Bend, Driftwood. The bars and shoals: Jones and Coconuts Reefs, Shagwong again. The fishing places: Frisbie's, Church's, Amsterdam, the Association, Tuma's, Tea House, Caswell's, Stony Brook, Greenbanks, De Milhau's. The places: Ram's Level, Hither Woods, Point Woods, Stepping Stones, Indian Jump, Split Rock, Water Fence, Quincetree Landing, Rod's Valley. The streams: Relie's Run, Ogden's Run. Montauk names, with few hints of the Montauks. It is as if, in taking the land— and the taking was more than two centuries in the doing—the old names had time to be forgotten as thoroughly as the Indian claims.

Chapter

XIX

THE THIRD AND ULTIMATE DIVISION of Montauk is a wedge pointing east from Great Pond, Fisher's Lake Montauk, a wedge two
and three-quarter miles wide at its base and tapering the same
distance toward the Lighthouse at the Island's end. Great Pond
was, until opened to Block Island Sound by dredging, another
lagoon formed by a bar along the Sound-front beach. It was
brackish and only occasionally open to salt water, sometimes
deliberately. My grandfather and his fellow fishermen would
dig a shallow trench along the beach and rig nets across the
rapidly widening outflow to catch wagonloads of fish, including,
they remembered, eels as thick as your arm.

   Now it is Lake Montauk, but still great in area if not in depth.
Much of its shallow bottom is privately owned, an anomaly going
back to the circumstances of Montauk's private purchase from
the Indians. This is a cause of thrown rocks between clam-
digging and scallop-dredging baymen and the owners of expensive waterfront homes, who assume that the lake's bottom and
the shellfish therein and thereon are theirs, and take umbrage

at the bayman's necessary habit of relieving himself (and herself, today) directly over the rail of the usual small skiff. "They are savages," a new resident told me, and before his dispute with the scallopers ended, a pistol and a knife, both unused, entered the argument on opposite sides. But this clash of cultures left unresolved the question of whether the owner of the bottom, who indubitably owns the clams resident within his ground, so to speak, also has a claim upon the scallops which frisk in the eel-grass midway between mud and air. Frisk? Yes, indeed, for scallops are self-propelled, and will travel thirty miles in a night and take up residence at Shelter Island if certain matters of shellfish etiquette and protocol are not observed by the baymen. This is a fact. It was told me by an elder of the tribe, whose dis-ability pension and movie career ended at the same time after the release of a short feature film produced by a young man with a long lens from the insurance company which pictured him haul-ing paired scallop dredges on a windy day at Three Mile Harbor.

East of Lake Montauk the ground slopes up into Indian Field toward Prospect Hill. Indian Field was where the Montauks hung on the longest, into this century, fighting in the courts their removal from the land until there were hardly any Montauks left.

Cattle grazed in Indian Field into the 1960s, overseen by herders from Third House, which was in the 1930s, '40s, and '50s Deep Hollow Dude Ranch. The pasture, now a county park, was rapidly overgrown with sumac, elder, oak, and black cherry when the grazing stopped. It was resumed on part of the land in 1977, but most of it remains new-wooded. Brooks run through the hollows and across some of the dirt tracks which are the only roads, the crossings providing what are probably the only fords with a small *f* on Long Island. To the east, toward Montauk Point and its granite lighthouse, built in 1796 at President George Washington's behest, the ground becomes rougher, with more and more small hollows, often floored with swamps or containing clumps of pepperidge, falling between steep little hills. South and east of Oyster Pond, real forest—"the Point Woods"—begins. Once it was "the Point Field," but today shadbush, whose white blossoms appear at the time of each spring's shad run and which despite its name grows to tree size, is interspersed with patches of holly. In winter the holly shows green through the beige of the woods, as does the laurel, poison to the sheep which once grazed Montauk more thoroughly than the cattle.

Here and there under Montauk's trees, from the great bulk of Split Rock back in Hither Wood out to the last wind-stunted growth below the bare carapace of Turtle Hill, which bears the Light itself, are boulders—glacial erratics, raisins and plums on and in the pudding moraine. Pushed along ahead of or within the glacier from New England or Canada, leaving their long scratches on the bedrock to the north, these great mica-flecked rocks have been rounded in the course of their journey. They attract legend or speculation; one, alongside Route 27 not far west of the Light, was painted around 1940 with the statement "Jesus Saves." The faded legend can still be read.

Those who read eternity into these rocks themselves are wrong. Every Rock of Ages has its cleft, or will have. In the cleft, moisture accumulates, and when the temperature drops below freezing the moisture expands with a great rending force, capable in time of cleaving the largest rock once, twice, many times. Tree roots work in the same manner and are wrenching away at Split Rock. Within the moraine, of course, are more rocks, waiting their turn to be uncovered, split, quartered, eighthed, and eventually turned into sand.

From the lump of moraine we call Turtle Hill, which was Wampanomon to the Indians and the Sag Harbor Lodge of Masons, which adopted the title, the next link of moraine in the chain, Block Island, is visible on a clear day. East of that lies Nantucket, then Martha's Vineyard, and then the hills of Cape Cod, all creatures of that last great glacier.

We were blackberrying, my grandfather and I, on the slope back of the site of the old Hither Plain Life Saving Station one day in the summer of 1944 or '45. The land was already part of the Mirror Development, a postage-stamp-lot real-estate promotion of the New York *Daily Mirror*, but we ignored the sign, the new houses, and the city people who sometimes yelled at us. Grandpa had picked there each summer since the early 1870s and had no intention of stopping. He had about filled his big thirty-six-quart carrier and I was wishing I was swimming, when another sort of buzz arose above the hum of the bees and pesky greenflies. The bushes around us were higher than a man's head; we could see only a meridianal patch of sky. The noise grew louder and louder and suddenly a man, seemingly perched on the end of a sort of girder below a whirling horizontal propeller, flew across our little sky, so low we might almost have jumped up and touched his feet.

"What in thunder was that?" Grandpa shouted as the noise died away. It was, we decided, a hel-io-copter, the first we had seen. The man was wearing a business suit; perhaps it was Igor Sikorsky himself, down from Bridgeport.

The hum of more conventional aircraft engines was long since familiar at Montauk. During World War I, Navy seaplanes were flown from a base at Fort Pond, and later dirigibles were tested there. In the Second War, a seaplane base at Rod's Valley on the west shore of Fort Pond Bay meant the end of the little seasonal settlement of pound-net fishermen there. But such things pass, and some never come to pass at all, like capitalist and railroad magnate Austin Corbin's long dream of a port of entry at Fort Pond Bay, great steamers saving a day's run on round trips to and from England, with fast passenger rail connections

MONTAUK LIGHT

(Corbin's) to New York, and freights (Corbin's) carrying coal out and cargo back. Such things pass, and Montauk remains, the compacted till of its bluffs eroding away at a pace far slower than the schemes of avarice.

From the top of the bluffs at Caswell's, the surfcasters' name for a stretch of rocky beach beyond Ditch Plain, Montauk Light is a small ringed finger, reddish band against pale flesh, raised in warning a mile or two to the eastward. On an unseasonable day in early spring, another one of Montauk's noises rises from the sea slowly heaving to the Atlantic's ground swell far below. A distant high-pitched sound, almost mechanical, like that of a spinning electric motor, it is the gossip of thousands of sea ducks —scoters mostly—flocked below, feeding on the small crustaceans of the rocky bottom. There are eiders here, too, and sheldrake diving closer to the big boulders along the shore. One does not hear the crash and wash of the breakers, only the music of the ducks.

There are surfers, young America in black wetsuits, coming out of the woods behind, blond hair bleached white by the sun. They clamber down the bluffs, which erode as much from the top as from the bottom, sliding in the loose sand and slipping over the greasy patches of clay. A Montauk surfcaster parked his Ford along here years ago, and when he returned he found the car on the beach below on top of a major slide of mixed moraine. People worry about the fate of the Light itself. Washington ordered it set far enough back from the brink to be safe for two hundred years, they say, and the two hundred years are about over. "Stop the erosion!" the cry goes up. But one man's erosion is another man's beach; if the flow of sand to the South Fork's ocean beaches is interrupted, there will be accelerated erosion to the westward, all the way to Coney Island. It's a puzzle, with no solution in sight, save that suggested by Robert Kennelly, a Southampton house mover, who would like a crack at moving the Light back from the sea. If the Egyptians can move the temples at Abu Simbel, he reasons, Bob Kennelly can move the Light. If other resort areas have fashionable, in-demand hairdressers or grocers, the South Fork has its house movers, and moving old buildings from point A to point B, for refurbishment and possible qualification for featureship in the Sunday *New York Times Magazine,* is an obsession of the eastern Long Island summer colony. One doubts that the popular Mr. Kennelly will ever get around to carrying off the Light to safety.

Moving buildings shoreward is all very well if there is land behind to move them to. Up at Fort Pond, where the East Hampton Town Trustees built a stone wall in 1820 (during a period in which they were trying to assert their authority over Montauk vis-à-vis the Proprietors) to keep the ocean out of the pond, there isn't much land left. An irascible Montauker of the civic watchdog breed, criticizing the public purchase of some ocean frontage there not long ago, calculated that Route 27, the main east-west highway, would be out on the beach before long. That would leave various buildings, including a supermarket, a dozen motels, and a busy real estate office, down there with the fishes. Perhaps.

The old-timers built farther back, like the late Joseph Loris, who long ago set up in the saloon business on the west shore of Fort Pond, "to sell whiskey to the soldiers." When I asked, "What war was that?" Mr. Loris offered, tentatively, "The Civil War?" but we did some calculating and decided it was the Spanish-American. He much resembled Edward G. Robinson, and I last saw him one winter's night when the barroom tables in his East Hampton Hotel had been pushed back for dancing, a gentlemanly octogenarian engaged in a stately two-step, unscarred by a long lifetime of lending an ear to and bouncing out drunks, and disputing the alcoholic beverage laws with a succession of Local Option, Prohibition, and State Liquor Authority agents.

Another friend now dead was Dave Howard, who served
with the Navy during World War II at the torpedo-testing station
on the site of the fishing village; the station's buildings now house
the Ocean Science Laboratory's investigations into the private
lives of lobsters and seaweeds. A Free French submarine dragged
anchor and came ashore during a winter northwest blow, one of
the usual three-day affairs, Dave recalled. "The seas were breaking right over her," he said, "and they had a little tiny tricolor
about the size of a pocket handkerchief flying off her conning
tower. The spray and the wind would tatter it in a couple of
hours and a Frenchman'd pop his head out of the hatch and run
up another one. Soon as the weather moderated, a tug came and
pulled her off and right out to sea they went, shot the man who'd
been on watch when she dragged, and threw him overboard."

Fort Pond Bay is as rugged as a French submarine skipper in
winter weather, and Montauk fishermen used great limber ash
spiles as mooring stakes for their small trawlers, derisively called
the Mosquito Fleet, there in the old days. The spiles bent, "gave,"
with the pounding seas. Even so, it was more than two decades
after the opening of Great Pond, its transformation into Lake
Montauk, and the establishment of docks there when the last
party boats left Fort Pond Bay. Politician Perry Duryea, a tradi-
tionalist if ever there was one, runs a lobster business at Fort
Pond Bay still, as his father and the Tuthills and Jake Wells did
before him. Perry, whose hair has gone white now and is known
in Albany as the Silver Fox, was once a baby like everyone else,
born at the family home near the lobster pound, and Dr. Dave
Edwards, Grandpa's brother and the man whose way had been
paid through medical school with the gold the *Shenandoah*
raiders missed, shot black duck on Tuthill's Pond below the
house while waiting for him to arrive.

That nativity was in Prohibition days, when Montauk was
nearly awash in rum, the voice of the Thompson submachine

gun was heard in the land, and the priest was said to have had difficulty in assembling a quorum for midnight mass among his largely French-Canadian fishing congregation, because all hands were down unloading a schooner. A certain Montauk raffishness predated the Volstead Act, however; a distant cousin of mine, celebrating the end of the Spanish-American War, is said to have fallen sound asleep up at the old inn on Signal Hill and to have been nailed into a coffin by convivial friends. They carried him down to the station and shipped him west with a freight-car-load of dead Rough Riders. He revived at Long Island City (where all changed in those years, even corpses, to the East River ferry), made himself known, and was rescued, to be restored to the bosom of his long-suffering but patient family.

Montauk bred other family stories. Doctor Dave's father and his bride were "going off" after their honeymoon in 1868 when the horse ran away with their buggy on Clapboard Hill, just west of the present Gurney's Inn, a resort and convention center of immodest proportions. Great-grandfather's leg was broken; his return from his wedding trip in such shape must have amused the Amagansett loafing element. The heavy crutch he made for himself and used while the leg mended—and used again when he grew old and lame, once to stump down the beach to be lifted into a whaleboat, from which he killed the last whale taken off Amagansett—hung in our barn in my boyhood. Clapboard Hill is still steep. When I go over it, I wonder what Great-grandfather would think of the motels. Not much, I suppose, but there is a good deal left at Montauk that his generation, and even the Indians who came before its members (and whom they resembled in many ways), would recognize, and find good.

Chapter

XX

Montauk Light could be seen from the top of the wedding-cake steeple of the Sag Harbor Presbyterian Church, they say, before the 1938 hurricane lifted Minard Lefever's ingenious concoction off the roof peak and smashed it down. The steeple, rising 187 feet above the ground, which is roughly fifty feet above sea level at that point, was built like a telescope, and each section, Greek, Roman, Chinese, Egyptian—Lefever was an architectural eclectic—was pulled up through the one below by block and falls, teams of oxen on the whip. The bell tolled as it fell.

The Light bears a shade south of due east by magnetic compass from the church, and twenty nautical miles separate the two. A line drawn between them would cross the high ground of Barcelona Neck, Alewife Brook Neck, Accabonac Neck, and North Neck, glacial hills rising 100, 130, and at Prospect Hill in Indian Field, Montauk, 160 feet above sea and bay level. The tip of the Light's cupola, above the lamp, is perhaps ten feet higher; the earth's curvature and the intervening hills are more than compensated for by the height of the church and the Light, which have more in common than their altitude, considerable as that is (or rather was) for the lowland landscape of eastern Long Island.

The Presbyterian steeple at Sag Harbor (the Old Whalers', some call the church today, assuming more than they ought to about the affiliation and piety of three or four generations of sea-men recruited from all quarters of the globe) was visible, too, from the mastheads of vessels coming in around Montauk and

ICE ON GARDINER'S BAY, 1934

bound for Sag Harbor in years gone by. In a time when even youngsters could name a brig or schooner by the trim of a yard or the cut of a topsail poking over the horizon, in an era when a whaling voyage might last four or five years, first sightings were more than occasions of sentiment. The keeper at Montauk Light would spot a returning whaler first, most likely, but by the time word got from Montauk to Sag Harbor—"The Port"—a vessel would, with any luck in wind and tide, have long since anchored east of Hog Neck or made her way in to Long Wharf, probably in whaling's heyday with the help of a steam tug.

The way to Sag Harbor, in a vessel of any draft, was around north of Gardiner's Point, where the Old Fort, built in 1898 to foil the Spaniards in any attempt to bombard Manhattan via the Sound and Hell Gate, molders today. There was no fort then, old or new, or any thought of one. The Point, now itself an island, was the lighthouse-occupied tip of a long, low sand spit running north from Gardiner's Island until the late 1880s, probably cut off by a breakthrough during the gale better known as the Blizzard of '88. South of Gardiner's Island, where the master had like enough taken on mutton and beef at the beginning of the voyage, years before, there was water deep enough for some whalers, but as they said then, it was pretty scant. I do not know when the narrow channel up past Promised Land and Ram Island shoal off Accabonac Creek was first buoyed, but even if it was marked in whaling days, the prudent captain of a long-legged vessel would have chosen the broad passage northward of Gardiner's Island, a passage used by the Royal Navy during the Revolution and the War of 1812.

The system of bays from Montauk to Sag Harbor, and beyond to the mouth of the Peconic River near Riverhead, Suffolk's county seat, is not much more than an irregular drowned valley between two great moraines, the Ronkonkoma of the South Fork and the Harbor Hill of the North Fork, and their associated out-wash plains and glacial deposits. Sag Harbor itself occupies such a deposit, a tangle of hills and hollows formed by the retreating glacier, much smoothed by time and modified by man. Rum Hill and its companions were shaved and bluffs made passable as the village grew, to a large extent upon salt marsh made into build-ing lots with fill taken from the slopes and peaks. The same process was used in the building of local roads, which, like the stretch over Clapboard Hill at Montauk, were once far more like roller coasters than they are today. To fill the hollows, material was taken from the crest, and the landscape was tamed; much of this work followed the automobile, which proved a great leveler in more ways than one.

Shelter and Gardiner's islands in the great V between the paired moraines are likewise offspring of the glaciers. Shelter Island has a marvelous morainal mound, the huge swell of hill behind Crescent Beach rising abruptly some 170 feet above Greenport Harbor. Gardiner's Island has a tamer topography, but its own distinction: Gardiner Clay, laid down as silt during an interglacial period. Back in the 1930s Zeb Tilton, the hero of Polly Burroughs' *Zeb: A Celebrated Schooner Life,* the Martha's Vineyard skipper of the *Alice Wentworth*, the last coaster in these latitudes, would, when he had nothing better to do and no other cargo in sight, work his vessel in against a little pier at the foot of the Gardiner's Island bluffs. There, with a wheelbarrow, a couple of shovels and whatever hard-working, sea-romance-stricken young man he had crewing for him at the time, he'd load the *Wentworth* with clay and amble her over to one of the New England pottery works. One such factory made toilets and sometimes shipped them aboard the *Wentworth*, which is why, if underwater archaeologists are wondering, part of the bottom of the harbor of refuge at Watch Hill, Rhode Island, is paved with commodes. The *Wentworth* dragged ashore in a blow, laden with modern conveniences, and was lightened in the most convenient way. My grandfather knew Zeb's brother, Captain George Fred Tilton, a notable Arctic whaler, but in Grandpa's view an unreliable yarn-spinner; I don't remember him ever mentioning Zeb, although he must have known this wall-eyed ox of a man from Sweet's Shipyard at Greenport, where the *Wentworth* was hauled regularly and in which my grandfather was a stockholder, and from the docks at Promised Land, where she sometimes loaded fish scrap. I remember seeing her there toward the end of her days, in the late 1930s, jibboom sticking far out over the oyster-shell-paved parking area at the foot of the Edwards Brothers dock.

Grandpa probably figured that Zeb, a reputed womanizer, was not a fit topic of conversation around children. Captain Tilton, like other seamen of the breed he outlasted, rarely bucked wind or tide. When the tide ran foul, he anchored and slept until it turned; he awoke on the turn when the skillet clanged on deck, having been pulled off the cabin table by a codline tied fast to a brick he had dropped overboard. He would heave in the brick (obtained from the brickyard he had supplied with sand dug off some flat during another spell without paying cargoes) and heave in his anchor and be off, wind or no wind, toward his destination.

The role of the tides in shaping waterfront geography is far more important than the inlander realizes, if he or she even thinks about the matter. The tide does not simply rise and fall like the red fluid in a barometer; it sets up strong currents, which usually run parallel to the trend of the shore. Back and forth the bay currents run, shaping a sand or earthen shore much as the potter's fingers shape moist clay. Without these currents, Long Island's shoreline would be, as are those of the almost tideless Baltic, irregular and dotted with small islands. With them, irregularities in any coastal landscape tend to be smoothed out, smeared together, as it were, by bars and beaches, except where the shoreline is mainly rock, as in Maine.

The speed of these currents is not great—one, two, and sometimes three knots, perhaps four miles per hour. The mass in motion, however, is awesome. Gardiner's Bay, San Diego Bay, Mobile Bay contain many millions of tons of water. All of the mass is in motion, gradually accelerating, flood-ebb, flood-ebb, four times a day, year in, year out, a prodigious natural force, one which might be thought capable of sweeping all before it.

Yet bars and shoals build or disappear at what is to us a gentle pace, although in geologic terms the changes in sandy bays and sounds are nearly instant.

Off eastern Long Island, in the warmer months at least, Zeb Tilton and anyone else working up or down the bay could rely on the afternoon breeze, "off the water"—that is, the Atlantic— from the southwest. The mechanics of this wind, regular enough in summer to set your watch by if you are not overpunctual, are simple. The sun warms the land, the air rises, and cooler air rushes in off the ocean to replace it. The cooler air carries the smoky haze of summer afternoons, or less romantically, con- densed moisture.

This reliable wind no doubt played a part three quarters of a century ago in the siting of the Devon Yacht Club at Amagan- sett. Quiet mornings and steady sailing breezes in the afternoon are the summer rule at Devon, which is only three quarters of a mile across the low expanse of Napeague Beach from the open sea. Tucked in the crook of the south end of Gardiner's Bay, Devon sailors sometimes have wind when there is a dead calm to the north and west. With the haze comes color, the yellow- gray light that attracted painters to the South Fork before the yachtsmen came. Childe Hassam used that light; so did William Merritt Chase; so does a new generation of East End painters today.

The blue-clear mornings turn into bronze-tinged afternoons, and the southwest breeze comes on, fitful at first, dark puffs cat's-pawing across glassy water. Some days it will struggle with a northwesterly at a shift-line off Springs, a little up Gardiner's Bay, patches of calm mixed with on-again, off-again gusts. Over on the Sound, between Long Island and the Connecticut shore and farther from the cool sea air, the irresolute summer wind drives sailors mad; in Gardiner's Bay the southwester generally prevails before long and holds sway until the land cools at dusk.

Headed up-bay under sail, the strong southwesterly will put
your boat's rail under as the breeze roars out over the low bars
separating bay from the creeks and harbors—Accabonac, Three
Mile, Northwest; there are lulls under the intervening bluffs at
Barnes Hole, Hog Creek Point, and Hedges Bank.

Off the creeks and hollows, sailors usually find deep water and
a clean bottom, but rocks left behind in the general retreat often
extend well offshore from the eroding bluffs. In some places
this withdrawal is less ancient than might be expected. During
the 1948 series of celebrations for East Hampton Town's Tri-
centennial (bicentennials are small potatoes on Long Island),
the hamlet of Springs treated itself to a clambake, on a field now
occupied by houses off King's Point Road in the Clearwater
Beach subdivision. Dr. Dave Edwards was the master of cere-
monies and made his usual joke: "I've seen a good many of you
before, some of you head-first, some of you feet-first, and some of
you bottom-first." His standing offer of $1,000 to the parents of
the first set of triplets he delivered had gone unclaimed for close
to fifty years then; a decade later, toward the end of his practice,
he missed his last chance when the three infant sons of an East
Hampton couple would not wait for him.

There was lobster and chicken and roast potato in addition to
the clams, and we ate at long tables borrowed from the church,
and thought about youth and antiquity. The field sloped down
through a swale toward the bay, providing a fine view of
Gardiner's Island, a good place to shoot black duck over corn
stubble in the fall of years gone by. In the foreground was, and
is, a rock about the size of a henhouse, a hundred yards offshore.
An ancient in attendance at the clambake recalled—"in Bonac,"
in the accent of Springs—that the boulder had stood at the edge
of the field in his boyhood, seventy-five years ago then and more
than a century ago now.

Across Gardiner's Bay to the northeast is Crow Shoal, the

southeast limit of the Royal Navy's fleet anchorage in the Revolution and the War of 1812, a flat where stumps have been exposed during abnormally low tides. There are stumps offshore at Napeague, too, and an entire island, Manhansack, in Shelter Island Sound not far from Sag Harbor, disappeared long ago. More recently Ram Island, also known as Cartwright Shoal,

ICEBOATING AT MECOX

south of Gardiner's Island, partially subsided beneath the water, which is now a foot or two deep at low tide where a few summers ago we picnicked and gulls stood watching, and where some summers before that ospreys built nests as high as a man's chest on the ground around a cattailed central swamp.

"South Ferry," the channel between Shelter Island and North Haven, formerly Hog Neck, could be waded by horses at low tide during the early years of the English settlement, according to tradition. There is forty-two feet of water there now. That Hog Neck is only one of several Hog Necks in these parts; there are many more Ram Islands than Cartwright Shoal, too. The Colonials were segregationists when it came to stock (when it came to people, preaching and practice went in slightly different directions; if blacks and Indians had to sit in the balcony at church, they managed to get together weekdays, and in a few generations the lines between red, black, and white were somewhat blurred), at least at certain seasons and most especially with gruff rams, rampageous hogs, and bellowing bulls, and small islands made suitable lockups for the lust-maddened creatures.

Chapter
XXI

THE POUND OF THE SURF and the sigh of the wind sometimes wake me before a fall dawn. By those sounds we could judge, when I was entering my teens, if it was weather for stringing for coots at Ram Island, at Cartwright. In my half-sleep, I am back in my grandparents' house on David's Lane, trying to guess from the murmurs of distant surf and chimney-top wind if the breeze will blow from the proper quarter and at the proper speed to allow my grandfather and his friends to shoot scoters from a long line of anchored rowboats in that corner of Gardiner's Bay.

This was, like most serious sports, largely ritual, as much a part of coming-of-age for me as joining the Presbyterian Church, and a good deal more interesting. It had begun, I suppose, around the turn of the century, when the first powerboats made it possible to tow fifteen or twenty sharpies, which are not much different from the sort of boat one rows around the lake in any city park, two or three miles north from the docks at Promised Land to The Shoals. It began, too, at a time when the East

Coast's supply of more palatable waterfowl—black duck, canvasback, and Canada geese—had declined.

It ended when the inevitable bastard offspring of that liaison between the internal-combustion engine and boats, the outboard motor, became reliable enough to lose the name "bastard" and worse. There was no longer any necessity for the communal effort involved in towing the sharpies, and the very presence on the bays of speeding outboards, sometimes bristling with shotguns in season, has made the great shoots of stringing days impossible.

Stringing involved a whole generation of men whom I knew in their last years. They were the old Long Islanders, mostly from Amagansett, East Hampton, Springs, and Wainscott, all of an age and most of them related in one degree or another. They had grown up on farms and around the water, although in profession they ranged from banker and doctor to the ne'er-do-well living off the gradual piecemeal sale of the family farm.

Some men of that generation were never invited. Some women of the next generation were, although they generally ran a launch down to leeward, picking up the dead birds and performing the chore euphemistically known as shooting over the cripples.

It wasn't that the women weren't good shots—most of them were excellent, products of that great emancipation of the 1920s and 1930s now forgotten—but it was a man's sport, although it never included those two masculinity props beloved of red-shirted deer hunters: the pint of whiskey and the dirty joke. It began with a man's breakfast, bacon and eggs and boiled coffee with eggshells in the pot. We set off for the Promised Land fishing docks well before dawn, frost underfoot some mornings and that strong coffee on our steamy breath. Grandfather's 1936 Dodge coupé pulled his four-wheel trailer, built on a Model A Ford chassis. On the trailer was lashed my sharpie, a thirteen-footer.

She had been a present, on my eighth birthday, I think, and was built in Amagansett by Tom Bennett, long dead now but still famous on eastern Long Island for his graceful yet utilitarian boats, which he signed with a branding iron: "T. Bennett— Amagansett."

The lapstrake sharpie, with cedar planks copper-fastened where they overlapped, was never named. She had a center-board trunk, and I learned to sail in her, steering with an oar. She had a cotton sail, cut in leg-o'-mutton style, longer in the foot than in the hoist, and I realized later that anyone who could handle such a rig could sail just about anything that floated. At the time, though, I thought it the handiest thing imaginable and delighted in running down on a set of range marks in Georgica Pond to trail a boat hook at exactly the right instant to pick up a string of crab traps I had dropped unbuoyed, lest the city people lift them and steal my blueclaws.

Inside the sharpie, on the road to Promised Land, were gener-ally piled two or three more boats, picked up at other gunners' barns as we went along. At the basin the boats were lifted off and stacked alongside the bulkhead, to be put overboard by Frank Smith, the patient dock and store manager for Edwards Brothers & Company. Mr. Smith had left his bed at five-thirty in the morning to sit in an outhouse-sized shed behind the clanking h'ister, a winch powered by an old auto engine and normally used to unload boxes of iced fish from the draggers and trap boats. He never shot, to my knowledge; but he was there when we went and there when we came back, armed with gently sardonic observations on the size of the bag relative to the volume of our distant cannonade.

One morning my sharpie, dangling below the long boom from a pair of box hooks under her gunwales, was dropped on top of a spile, which went clean through alongside the centerboard trunk. Mr. Smith was apologetic, and George Davis, a carpenter and a duck-shooting friend of my grandfather's, replanked her a few days later. It was not a difficult job, since, unlike just about everything else that floats, a sharpie is cross-planked, so he simply ripped out the damaged planking, nailed in new, and sawed off the ends.

That sharpie had bad luck; I had hardly been given her when she slid on the trailer as we were en route to Alewife Brook, crabbin', and her port side was split open against an oak. Later, one morning at Cartwright Shoal, my Remington twelve-gauge semi-automatic, one of the first made and old then, jammed. "Here," Grandpa said, and he took the gun to pound the butt of its stock against the bottom of the boat. The butt came down across the hammers of his ten-gauge double, which rested with its muzzle over the thwart at the stern sheets. Both barrels discharged and blew to smithereens the port-side natural-crook knee where side met transom.

"Don't tell your mother," Grandpa said mildly. Another day someone else shot a hole through the bottom of his sharpie, but he stuffed a mitten or a sock in the cavity and kept on gunning.

The boats were assembled in the Promised Land basin and made fast like links in a sausage, painter-to-stern, painter-to-stern. When all was ready, we piled aboard whatever boat was tug that day and found a spot to sit in the lee. Sometimes it was my great-uncle Sam Edwards's *Tad*, a sturdy cabin cruiser known as the Turd to some of the less reverent fisherman customers at Edwards Brothers, who thought she took up useful space in the basin. Sometimes it was an old Coast Guard motor surfboat belonging to the village jeweler and watch repairman, aboard which he died some summers later and drifted for a day with his distraught wife, my kindly Sunday School teacher, whom he had never taught to start the engine. Once or twice it was one or the other of the Edwardses' small fleet of 110-foot trawlers, which were former Navy subchasers and were, in typical Edwards fashion, four or five sizes too large for the job. It was a family trait, like using ten-penny nails where sixteen-to-the-penny would do, or so many bunkers that the hill of corn withered and died.

Whoever was towing, there would usually be a great snarl of boats or a fouled propeller in getting out of the basin. This resolved, we would steam off to The Shoals, hooking around its southwest end and through the unmarked channel, which seems to follow that sand bar whatever its migrations, and drop off the gray-painted boats one by one a scant gunshot apart in an anchored skein paralleling Ram Island, the dry portion of The Shoals.

The line of boats, perhaps twenty of them at intervals of roughly two hundred feet, sometimes stretched nearly a mile across what must once have been one of the world's great feeding grounds for sea ducks. There is from ten to sixteen feet of water over this broad submerged plateau. On or in the bottom grow the clams, mussels, periwinkles, moon snails, slipper shells (quarter-decks, deckuhs, to the Bonacker) which comprise the diet of the sea ducks, divers one and all.

This is a lonely place, greenish water, blue sky, a little yellow sand in the offing on Ram Island or Cartwright proper, and in those days, the fish-hawk nests, piles of twigs and rubbish three or four feet high but looming taller in the horizontal seascape. The hills of Gardiner's Island, brown in gunning season, are too far away to impose. For two or three years during World War II, there were sand pyramids bulldozed up over the osprey nests on Cartwright, targets for the machine guns, rockets and bombs of steel-blue Grumman fighters, which flew low over the string of boats once, pilots waving cheerily.

On our approach, coots, scoters of three varieties—the white-winged, the surf, and the black—and their companion old squaws would buzz off like angry bees, to swarm up to the northwest and down to the southeast, over the line of The Shoals, until all the sharpies were in place and still. Then the birds would come back, low lines six and eight feet above the water, whipping along to flare higher as they crossed the line of boats. *Whump!* would go the first gun, a deeper noise than that produced by today's gunpowders, although that may be recollection playing me tricks. A duck would tumble, and all hands would cheer.

The usual shot was at a single passing bird or a small bunch. As the coots approached we would bend at the waist, as low as we could, and remain still, eyes rolled up to peer out from under the brim of what was often a round canvas gunning cap, shaped like a sailing hat, of a style popular for nearly a century among gunners but no longer made. One such was the favorite hat of my childhood, in fact the only one I would wear, and I remember the tears rolling down my cheeks in Rogers, Peet as a saleslady fit an Eton cap to my head at my mother's orders.

We sat frozen. Some say sea ducks can be tolled—that is, summoned—by waving a flag or a hat, and I've seen it done, but we sat still, and hoped. If the bird came close enough—and judging distance over the water is one of the secrets of waterfowling—the shot was always from a sitting or kneeling position, since standing was an invitation to a capsize. The shot was often more or less over the shoulder as one swung and was prevented from turning the lower torso by the boat's appropriately named thwart, or seat.

Shooting from such positions, the gunner is of necessity hunched to his work, back, neck and head in a long curve down to the barrel of his gun. I've never seen a photograph that caught it, although there is a Currier & Ives print of an Indian in deep snow shooting at a wolf or deer that has the deadly awkward stance exactly.

Swing, lead, squeeze. With a clean shot, the duck would appear to trip in midair, tumble to the water, splash and float belly up, dead. A miss was more likely, or a winged bird that would go down, to be chased and shot again, often diving and coming up behind the boat or, sometimes, diving and never coming up again. In this instance the duck was said to have seized seaweed in his bill and drowned himself rather than give up to his tormentor. I think this is true; I have seen dead coots come to surface with strands of rockweed in their bills, a haunting sight and a memory that leaves me in wonder that I ever was as infatuated with hunting as with girls, and in the same years.

Kneeling, one's knees would be protected by hip boots from the water that was almost always in the bottom of the boat. It seems, in retrospect, as if every male on eastern Long Island clumped along in hip boots in those days. Ashore, they were turned down once, to the knee, with the top half hanging loose to the ankle, enhancing the swagger that went with the boots. I was laid up in Southampton Hospital with pneumonia once back then, in a room down the hall from the children's ward. There was a Montauk boy there, younger than I and more or less raised aboard his father's dragger. I could hear his stories being told to the other youngsters, and from their tone and content I know he was wearing his boots in bed. Most of the baymen today wear waders instead of boots; perhaps, too, in these more prosperous times, there are more shoes for dry-land wear around. In any event, hip boots are in a decline.

Coot shooting was work for expert gunners, and even they probably fired three or four shells (generally twelve-gauge, with the heavy ten-gauge still used by a few traditionalists and the sixteen by a couple of modernists) for each duck killed. Then, too, for every duck picked up, there was probably another drifting away toward Montauk dead or mortally wounded.

A coot, separated from his bunch, might fly the length of the line, winning a cheer when missed by the successive fire of a dozen or more guns. Another might cross and recross, finally to be hit. Once or twice I saw gunners hit by falling birds; there was little room for dodging in a sharpie. Those birds that splashed nearby we would retrieve ourselves, throwing over a buoyed anchor warp to be picked up on rowing back to weather. No one brought a dog along except Captain Sam, whose Sport, as each member of his long series of spaniels was named, was generally aboard whatever big boat we had along. The Sport of my teens was locally famous for his ability to ferret out the single half-pound butterfish, a species to which he was addicted, in a deck-load of porgies. Birds that fell at a distance were picked up by the powerboat.

A loon, which was indelicately known on Long Island as a shitepoke, might cross, and once or twice I saw one shot by an old-timer scornful of the law and craving the flavor, which is said to be memorable. A few sheldrake, that is, mergansers, were usually in the mound of dead ducks piled later at Promised Land, a dark heap which numbered two and three hundred birds at times. No one cared much for sheldrake, although in later years my great-uncle Doctor Dave acquired a taste for them and a common Long Island nickname, Sheldrake, from his contemporaries who knew this secret vice. They maintained that his salivary apparatus had degenerated from age, and that sheldrake was the only food strong enough for him to taste. He just laughed, knowing better. Uncle Dave didn't look like a human sheldrake; most who had the nickname were angular-faced, with swept-back hair like the duck's crest.

Uncle Dave introduced us to coot steak—the breasts, soaked in salty water to remove the blood, cooked rapidly on an almost red-hot, dry salted griddle or frying pan. He once caused a family row by challenging his sister-in-law, my grandmother, to tell the difference between coot cooked this way and venison steak.

At a dinner party she failed the test and argued that he had cheated and cooked venison. Grandma was a coot cooker and had in her time dispatched them by the thousand over a succession of coal, coal oil, and gas stoves, and should have known the difference. But she was wrong, for her dish was coot fricasseed or stewed, a different kettle of fish-duck.

In stringing for coots, decoys were rarely used, although now and then someone would bring along a few silhouettes arranged to float on a frame and give him an edge over the other gunners. The sheldrake shooter, crouched in a pit along one of the bay beaches, with southerly or southeast wind at his back and flat water in the lee of the land offshore, would need them, and a retriever, too. The old sheldrake decoys are almost serpentine, catching the reptile-thrust of the merganser neck while swimming on the feeding grounds and its low body. There is something shamanistic about duck decoys, which seem to have been exclusively North American at least until recent times. The earliest ones are Indian, excellent shapes in bent and bundled reed found in dry caves in the hills above the tule lakes of Nevada, some painted and some trimmed with feathers, but unmistakably decoys.

Weekenders out from Manhattan walking the Sagaponack potato fields one foggy fall day came upon a field full of feeding geese, looming large in the murk. They approached the birds, which stood still and silent. Aha, they said; decoys. As they got closer they could see the very feathers, wings, bent necks, bills. The hair rose on their necks as they realized they stood in a flock of forty or fifty real geese, stuffed and wired into feeding shapes by some manic taxidermist as decoys. They returned the next day for a better look, and the geese were gone. The decoy is a powerful totem.

Perhaps once a season we coot shooters would string off the

ocean beach, a delicate operation requiring both real weather knowledge on the part of the graybeard leaders of such expeditions and a perfect day, with a northwest wind to flatten the Atlantic surf.

On one of these ocean expeditions Doctor Dave did bring along a set of stool. Landing through the surf at the end of the morning in an eight-foot decked duckboat, deep-laden with a shotgun, iron shell box, a bunch of dead coots, and his decoys, he capsized. He was immediately tangled in the decoy lines, each with a small lead anchor on its end, and by the time he got clear and retrieved his gear, he had swallowed a good deal of cold salt water and was a candidate for pneumonia, which he achieved. Any one of his patients of his age, which was then around seventy, who had done the same would have been on the receiving end of one of his frank and stentorian lectures.

Those shoots in the ocean, off the Main Beach in East Hampton, Indian Well Plain Highway at Amagansett, or once, on a memorable occasion, twelve or fifteen miles to the eastward at Ditch Plain, Montauk, had a different quality from the Gardiner's Bay affairs. Perhaps it was the ocean swell, apparent even on the calmest days. In the late 1940s I was given a small outboard motor, the only one in the flotilla ordinarily, and was dispatched east or west as the set was running, to pick up the dead and wounded ducks.

To be alone on the ocean in the late fall was an experience. I wonder if I would let my oldest boy, now about the age I was then, do it, or indeed what I would say if he announced that he wanted to take up duck shooting. Yet although I never saw a life jacket in any of the boats, no one worried, and no one had ever drowned at stringing, so far as I knew. It was an excellent school for small-boat handling, and most of those who went along had fished commercially at least briefly in their lives. Almost all of the old-timers, who had grown up before the turn of the century in a place surrounded by salt water, had done so, and perhaps half of those senior coot shooters had improved upon fishing and had been shore whalers.

Chapter
XXII

GARDINER'S BAY WAS FOR US a place of warm-weather fishing, clamming, swimming, and sailing, too. It came as a surprise to learn that New England yachtsmen, entering that body of water from Long Island Sound through Plum Gut, a boisterous strait northwest of Gardiner's Point, or from the shallows west of Napeague Bay, considered it dangerous. Yet it is, and more so in the fall and winter—the gunning season—than yachting time. Years after our stringing expeditions to Cartwright Island and The Shoals, three young men were drowned there while coot shooting, unaccompanied and late in the season. They were experienced boatmen, but their boat drifted into the gut north of Cartwright and capsized, with no one within sight to help. Its outboard motor fell off and anchored the boat by the control cables squarely in the rough water of the gut, where wind met tide, and they drowned in heavy clothing. Relatives came up from Montauk in other boats and spent Christmas crisscrossing that part of the bay in search of their bodies.

There is a risk simply in being on the water in a small boat in

fall or winter, of course. One day in the late 1950s, three or four
of us decided to go stooling—shooting over decoys—in Northwest
Harbor, back of Cedar Point. We must have had a late start, for
it was getting on toward dark when we headed home, the two-
cylinder Michigan in my catboat *Old Torrup* thumping along.
We had John Collins' little dory in tow, a boat long since gone
to pieces, although she was around for many years and at one
time or another belonged to just about everyone in the area who
liked to fool with old boats, and her gaff-headed rig lives on in
an ancient yawl boat.

There we were, out in Gardiner's Bay, with the wind picking
up, blowing a gale out of the northwest before long. We were
headed for Three Mile Harbor running to leeward, and the
dory's painter snapped once, twice, thrice. It was pitch-dark the
third time, and the long sand bar called Sammy's Beach was
close under our lee. John jumped in the dory as we tried to make
fast again, and shouted that we should let him drift ashore, but
we made another try. The catboat was in shoal water by this time,
and a sea broke clean into the big cockpit of the *Old Torrup*,
which was eleven feet in beam and just twice that in length. She
was spongy as an old basket, and had she struck on that hard
sand bottom, it would have been the end of her, although we
probably would have made the beach. The engine sputtered but
kept going, and we got a line to John.

We clawed off and made Three Mile Harbor's entrance
channel. Here, trouble would have been final. The tide was
ebbing fast, so fast that we made hardly any headway against the
huge standing waves pushed up in the narrow thoroughfare as
the ebbing tide battled the northwest blow at our stern. Slowly
we inched in, wrestling the barndoor rudder, watching for stubs
of piling from the decaying west jetty by the intermittent light
of the flasher on the stone jetty opposite, and hoping the little
Michigan would continue its patient beat.

We were safe at the dock when I remembered that my grandfather and two or three of his brothers had come close to going for their last long swim from another catboat in Gardiner's Bay perhaps half a century earlier, on a similar winter night. They were coming back from shooting on Gardiner's Island, under power, and one of them—Uncle Bert, I think—was down below when rising water woke him up. The boat had hit a log or wreckage, but they found the hole, stuffed it tight with a coat, and got home.

The Edwardses gunned a lot on Gardiner's Island in those days, when F. Augustus Schermerhorn and later Clarence H. Mackay "had the shooting from the Gardiners" under lease. This was long before Mr. Mackay's daughter Ellin ran off with a song writer named Irving Berlin, to the amazement of Society. Grandpa, to whom Berlin was a place inhabited by damned Dutchmen, once swung on what he thought was a goose during a snowstorm at Great Pond on Gardiner's Island and came up with a swan. "Some good eatin'," he assured me. Years later we spent a morning sloshing through the Dreen south of the Nature Trail preserve in East Hampton Village, one from each end, in armed pursuit of a great blue heron he'd seen there, a breed he recalled from his childhood as tasty. The bird had flown the swamp, I'm pleased to report.

The Edwardses' presence on Gardiner's Island during the days of leased shooting was not social; they were hired to carry guests back and forth in their fishing boats, and they acted as guides. In years when the deer had become so plentiful that food was scarce and they ran to runts, the local men would take part in drives down toward The Shoals. The whitetails would be pushed in numbers out onto the barren bar and shot with rifles from pits. The pits were for safety, to help keep the gunners from hitting one another, and the dressed deer would be carried away by boat, to be sold to New York restaurants.

Mortality was confined to the ducks during our communal coot-shooting voyages, despite the danger inherent in shotguns and small boats, particularly in combination. The worst thing that ever happened while stringing was "gettin' peppered." One expedition took place on a school day, and I went down David's Lane in East Hampton at noon to find out from Grandpa how it had gone. He was sitting shirtless at the dining-room table pretending to read the stock tables in the *Times*, and Grandma was in a chair alongside, lips pursed as she pried Number Four shot, lead pellets about a sixteenth of an inch in diameter, from Grandpa's flank with the points of her sewing shears.

Now and again she would sterilize her instruments over a candle. "Lew Parsons did it," Grandpa said with a grin. Lew was a contemporary and a friend from boyhood; he built and lived in a charming late-Victorian house that remains an ornament of Amagansett. "He must be getting near-sighted," Grandpa observed.

Lew was a tall man, a little stooped, with a kindly smile; sure enough, he wore glasses. He was also, it developed after his death at a great age, a compulsive saver of this and that, the sort of person who used to be pictured in *Life* magazine rolling along his life's work, a thousand-pound ball of tinfoil. His executors were rumored to have found vast sums of money in small packets taped to the undersides of drawers and on top of cellar water pipes. Bill Durham, who bought the property, cleared out the Parsons stable for use as a painting studio, making trip after trip to the town dump with crates of second-hand washers, bottle caps, worn-out shoes, and the like. His prize find was a large and heavy box, correctly marked "String, Under Six Inches."

Grandpa had been wearing a heavy leather jacket the day Lew Parsons winged him, but the shot, as I could see, were pretty well into him, a quarter-inch and more. Grandma got them all; Grandpa hated to bother Dave, his doctor brother, with minor problems. He was less contemplative later that fall, however, when his old friend Lew got him again, under similar circumstances. I was in the boat with him that time, and unhit, although I heard some lively language. Grandpa was president of East Hampton's one-horse water utility, the Home Water Company; Lew was treasurer of its Amagansett counterpart (Grandpa's youngest brother, Captain Sam, was its president), and perhaps some subliminal business rivalry was at work.

A few years later Grandpa was dead, the Suffolk County Water Authority was buying up all the small utilities, and I was alone in the sharpie off Amagansett when the man in the next boat in the string of a dozen or so, a Manhattan sportsman of note, swung in my direction. I saw the flash and as I ducked toward the gunwale I felt a sharp slap on the right side of my head. There was caked blood at the corner of my eye and behind my ear when we got ashore, and I walked up to the man and reported that he had got me pretty good. He turned a cold eye, said he had been shooting for thirty years or more without having done such a thing, and walked away.

The shot, two of them, are in there still. Grandma was alive then (in fact, a year or two later, she coaxed me into knocking off a cock pheasant out of season across David's Lane, a 1920s residential street cut through her Uncle David Huntting's back lot, with a .22 target rifle fired out the front entrance of her house while she held the door open, and was later caught picking the fowl clean down cellar by a meter reader, which amused him and embarrassed her), but I didn't feel up to a session with her shears and candle.

The stringing crowd didn't think much of those who engaged in similar pass shooting along the curve of the Cedar Point beach in those days. "Moonshooters"—those who futilely banged away at ducks far out of gunshot—were said to be the rule there, and Cedar Point gunners, even though generally ensconced like the

Gardiner's Island deer-drive killers in deep pits like foxholes, were said to run a real risk of being shot in the dangerous sense—that is, at close range—as opposed to being peppered from a distance. A shotgun blast from close in is murderous, at a hundred yards or more generally a nuisance, albeit a painful one.

Not always, however. East Hampton did, in the late 1960s, lose a leading citizen to a shotgun charge at such a range. The gun, a gift to a lady from the victim, for her self-protection, was fired in the moonlight by a rival suitor, and the wounds, although relatively trivial, brought on a fatal heart attack.

What the old-timers meant about Cedar Point, although they never put it into words (there was a great deal understood about this and other matters that they never put into words), was that the pit gunners lacked a certain sense of decorum, of style, which could be required and enforced when the effort, like an expedition to Cartwright Shoal, was necessarily a group endeavor under the direction of grave seniors.

We had heard, we youngsters—and there were a few others besides myself who had been extended the Cartwright privilege—that East Hampton Town Police Chief Harry Steele, already renowned to us as a World War I pilot and powerful authority figure when all 220 pounds of him was dressed in blue, goggled and tucked aboard an Indian motorcycle, had once bagged a flying coot with his .38 revolver at Cedar Point, and we wished we had seen the feat. But when we were old enough to have our own cars (mine a 1933 Plymouth roadster painted duck-boat gray, with dark-green trim) and sneaked off to Cedar Point, we didn't tell about it.

Cedar Point, like the Home Water Company, has now been taken over by Suffolk County, and shooting in the park is carefully supervised and said to be as good as anything about, with the exception of such private preserves for the wealthy sportsman as Mashomack on Shelter Island or Gardiner's Island. The

Cartwright shooting, like a great deal of public hunting in the United States, was done in by the galoots who decimated flocks of coots from speeding outboard boats for a decade and more, by the oil spills that have taken a heavy toll among all the North Atlantic seabirds, and, yes, by stringers who killed coots by the hundreds on Saturday mornings for the first half of this century. There are scoters, and old squaw and eider, in great numbers off Montauk each winter now, but the flocks in Gardiner's Bay, along the South Shore beaches and up and down the East Coast generally are tiny in comparison with what they were. One little flock feeds winter and summer at the south end of Gardiner's Bay. It includes four or five coots, all cripples; none can fly, although they dive for their food. One has a stub wing, which it flails after each dive, as if in pain. These ducks cannot migrate and simply swim out to open water when the bay freezes there, as it does nearly every winter.

Were there sea ducks in plenty, I would not shoot them now. I began to change, I think, one fall day seventeen or eighteen years ago when I went alone to Cartwright in the catboat, towing the Tom Bennett sharpie. I had made a dozen old squaw stool, to see if they would toll the birds as much as anything else, and I set them out from the sharpie, leaving the catboat anchored off in the distance. The stool floated like a small feeding flock, and they worked.

A pair of old squaws came tearing up, and I knocked one down, a female. The tide was slack, there was no wind, and she drifted among my new decoys. Her mate—I know old squaws are not monogamous, but he was a drake—came back and circled, wings whistling. He circled again, and I knocked him down. I looked around; I was all alone in the center of barren bay and vacant sky. I picked up the stool and the dead ducks and headed home.

The wooden old squaws are stacked in the barn alongside

sheldrake, brant, and black duck, all with their anchor lines wrapped around them and their lead or cast-iron anchors in place. I've shot ducks, a few, since then, and when a goose comes tacking along the dunes at Napeague in a blow, I find myself tempted to run for the double-barreled twelve-gauge Stevens that replaced the balky Remington, but the last little gunning I did was for the pot, the table having come to outrank sport in my priorities. Then, too, there has been enough killing in the world. My father, who never hunted after he came back from France, where he was one of Pershing's Army hospital orderlies (and made friends with an idealistic young one-legged German prisoner who became a Nazi in the 1930s; end of friendship), and from post-revolution Russia, told me that long ago.

He was gone, like his coot-stringing, swan-shooting father-in-law, before I believed him. But I don't begrudge others hunting, or regret those long-ago mornings at The Shoals. If it is to be done, though, it ought to be done with what those old-timers never called style, although that is what it was, a quality that seems to be in short supply these days.

Chapter
XXIII

IF GARDINER'S BAY has been taking from the land, it has been giving at about the same rate. Cedar Island, south of the channel into Sag Harbor, where the government established a lighthouse to guide the whalers in and out as early as 1839, was truly an island until this century. Today it is nothing more than the tip of the pit gunners' peninsula (which sports a few lonely cedars). Gardiner's Point, now an island, is the reverse of this. My mother used to visit her friends the Mulford girls on Cedar Island in the early 1900s. She had to row across a considerable strait to get to the Light. Keeper Mulford was a Civil War veteran with a wooden leg; the leg, or one of his spares, was in the commodious attic of the granite lighthouse the last time I looked, in the early 1960s. Since then the building has been thoroughly vandalized and partially gutted by arsonists, and the leg has no doubt joined its Keeper in Heaven.

At the south end of Cedar Point, on the Northwest Harbor side, where the deep water runs in close to the bank and a menhaden plant fumed in the late 1800s, East Hampton's first port—

the original Northwest Landing, as opposed to the present small-boat harbor two miles to the westward—may have been established shortly after the settlement. The argument over the site is a matter about which reasonable people may differ: Was the Town Wharf here, between Alewife Brook and the base of Cedar Point, where the old "Road to the Landing terminated," or down by the present Landing?

The matter is over three hundred years old now, and no one knows for sure. We do know that the establishment of Sag Harbor a hundred years after East Hampton's settlement and the subsequent building of its Town Wharf meant a rapid end to trade at Northwest. The course of commerce has never been a steady upward curve, and there are many such once-ports, now nearly forgotten, on the Atlantic and Pacific coasts, ports rendered obsolete by changing cargoes, draft requirements of shipping, or the opening of new routes. So, too, are there once-bustling inland commercial centers with grass growing in their streets, victims of the decline of the railroads, the end of steamboating on the inland rivers, the decay of the canal system, or, finally, the routing of the superhighways.

At East Hampton, scattered farms around the Northwest port lingered on, less and less prosperous as the soil of the deposits became more and more depleted of the nutrients accumulated through millennia of forest mulch, until this century.

The farmsteads are marked today by cellar holes, irregular depressions picked over by bottle hunters, and stone-lined wells half filled with debris turned into soil, which are homes to timorous garter snakes. Old orchards are signaled by battered apple or pear trees, their blossoms in April and May joining with the shad and dogwood to streak the oak and pine grays and greens of Northwest Woods with white. Along the bluffs, the beach plum contributes to the decoration, sometimes with a peach-pink bloom.

On the north-facing beach the glacial boulders are in a rough row, as if they had been pushed by the winter's ice, as well they may have been. Logically they would not have fallen thus, half-way between the low, eroded bluff and the ebb-tide line, if they were merely the vertically dropped deposit of washed-away glacial till. They very often come in pairs, two-, three-, or four-foot boulders of the same shade and consistency, split halves of the parent rock. This is the beach whose possession Josiah Kirk disputed with the East Hampton Town Trustees all through the years between 1861 and 1881. At issue was the collection of seaweed for fertilizer; the land was eroding, and Kirk, an outlander, foreign to East Hampton and its ways, claimed the beach and its seaweed as his, out to its former bounds. He spent his fortune in the courts, won his case, and died in the almshouse.

Back in the woods behind the remains of Josiah Kirk's once-prosperous farm, one large cellar hole with many bricks and half a dozen smaller ones lined with stone, are two small ponds, watering holes for the cattle. Near one is an old hedgerow and ditch, the surface much lower on the farm-pond side from the tramping of the milling herds. Back in the woods, toward the Peach Farm, where East Hampton's leading still was uprooted during Prohibition, is the Buffalo Waller, where the Gardiners' pet buffalo and cattalo wallowed in the mud at the turn of the century. This was an experiment of David Gardiner, who had the tombstone in his cellar floor and anticipated recent efforts to breed a beef animal capable of living off the land. He mated cattle with bison he had personally collected in the West. When they were put out in the Gardiner pasture at East Hampton Village, the shaggy offspring were teased by youngsters fleet enough to escape over stout barbed-wire fences; running wild in Northwest Woods, the cattalo wreaked their revenge by disrupting summer picnics. The last buffalo finally went to the Bronx Zoo; the cattalo presumably went the way of good beef.

Traffic over the Northwest Woods bluffs does not always contribute to their diminution, heretical though this sounds, given the ecologists' views on the care of dunes. In some instances, particularly when bay dunes or bluffs front north, human passage on foot or in vehicles results in a rapid build-up of wind-blown sand on top of and to the rear of the crest. One dune line along Gardiner's Bay was frequently crossed in a certain spot by haul-seiners' four-wheel-drive trucks. A gap quickly developed; through it the northwest gales pushed tons of fine sand. In a few years a raised dikelike road, trailing off to the southeast on the back of the dune some eight feet above the original grade, gradually curved down to end a good hundred feet inland.

The blowing-sand phenomenon has been repeated on the bluffs on the north side of Hither Hills State Park at Montauk, facing Block Island Sound and the East Coast's strongest steady winter wind, the northerly gale. Here, persons climbing up and running down have cut the lip of the bluff. Fine glacial sand from its face is blown up and over, back into the low wind-trimmed oaks, piling up into great yellow-orange dunes which sometimes top the bluff by fifteen and twenty feet. The sand, coming from the bluff-face, has never been washed by salt water, and unlike the white sand of the beach below, has not lost its iron-oxide tint.

From Cedar Island Light, Mashomack Point on Shelter Island is a short canoe paddle. The Montauks and the Manhansets are said to have traveled and traded on this route, down Cedar Point and over the rolling hillocks along the west side of Three Mile Harbor, across the higher ground and through the oak forest toward Amagansett, to emerge onto the Indian Well Plain about where the village begins today, and on to Montauk, by way of the beach in mosquito time. Shelter Island's Quakers traded too; vessels carried timber and dried cod to the West Indies, returning with rum and salt, and some good-sized hulls were built in some unlikely places on their island, as on the banks of narrow

West Neck Creek, a tidal stream winding in from Peconic Bay a mile and more northward into a deep circular pond, making a perfect anchorage then and now.

Much as the bay shore has eroded here and built up there, man's commerce has shifted, from Northwest Landing to Sag Harbor, from West Neck to Stirling (now Greenport), the

CEDAR ISLAND LIGHT

North Fork hamlet which blossomed into a seaport in the early nineteenth century and was the easterly terminus of the Long Island Rail Road in the years before tracks were laid to link New York and Boston. At Greenport, travelers bound for New England disembarked from "the cars" and boarded a steamer.

Our concern with nature has generally been limited to immediate questions: If tracks can't be laid across rocky, rolling Connecticut, can we run them down Long Island to Greenport? Is there depth of water there for the steamer? Will the farmers ship by rail, and can they grow enough to make it worthwhile? Along the shoreline, public interest in what the colleges call geology varies in more or less direct proportion to erosion, which is what we call the building up of someone else's beach when the sand comes from in front of our house. Bay-front erosion became a source of property-owner concern in the 1950s and 1960s, when a combination of natural circumstances spurred erosion, which brought about certain rapid changes in topography—changes no one would have noticed had not the disappearing topography been topped by new houses. Bluffs began to erode, and when they were bulkheaded at their bases, the beaches below, starved of their usual nourishment from the sliding bluff-face, disappeared. In the 1950s the Army Engineers held hearings into the problem, and old-timers testified that surge and storm tides along the Greenport waterfront had been greatly intensified by the permanent breakthrough at Gardiner's Point seven decades earlier, during the Blizzard of '88, and ten miles to the eastward.

No doubt they were right, but was the surge, the resonant action of faraway waves amplified into slow but weighty pulses of the water, "worse" or merely "greater"? Nature works around the clock; little is constant or forever, not even the vernal return of the alewife to the brook back of Cedar Point which bears her name, and to myriad other brooks and runs up and down the coast. The dictionary is uncertain about this herring's name; she is deep-bellied, perhaps that is the derivation. Or perhaps the word is Anglicized Indian. One thing is known: the fish used to be called Ely, for the East Hampton Town records of the seventeenth century—taken down with quill pens by men with excellent ears, and despite their Roundhead heritage, a truly Cavalier attitude toward the conventions of spelling—had the word that way, and it is still pronounced so on eastern Long Island, and sometimes spelled so too, as on East Hampton Town road signs today.

Alewife Brook meanders like the channel leading into Pond of Pines eight or ten miles away at Napeague, although on a grander scale. The brook's twists and turns and travels across the marsh are like those of a mountain stream in a beaver meadow, and follow the same rules of progression—deep water on the outside of a curve where water velocity is greater, shoals building out on the inside of a curve, and eventual cutoffs—the rules obeyed by all streams, from little Alewife Brook, less than a mile long, to the great Mississippi. Alewife Brook, however, outdoes the Father of Waters in one respect: it is tidal, changing direction four times a day and complicating the equation beyond imagination.

The alewife herself, the only fish I know whose pursuit is as well carried out with a washtub as with a rod, is small and bony, not really worth the trouble to eat unless it is pickled long enough to dissolve the bones, in which case the common fish becomes a rare delicacy. "Too bony" is, of course, what they once said about the shad, whose roe now goes for $4 a pair. Salmon, formerly so common that indentures were said to have carried a clause prohibiting the feeding of the fish to servants "bound" by such agreements more often than once a week, are gone from most of the Northeast's rivers. It is an event when a passing stray is caught in a gill net off Long Island, and even then, scientific examination is likely to pronounce the trophy a sea-run brook trout.

Some fish wax and wane in numbers to no apparent rhythm; bluefish are now in a period of relative plenty, more abundant than at many periods in the past; bass seem to be in a decline. The weakfish have returned, some believe because of the ban on

DDT. Blowfish, or puffers, are scarce, perhaps because of good prices and resultant overfishing. They were thrown away as unmarketable, or given to the children to skin (using as their only implement a finishing nail driven halfway into a board, a rapid procedure astounding to the amateur who has attempted the wrestling of the sandpaper hide off a reluctant victim who is huffing himself up to soccer-ball size and shape) and sold as candy money, not so long ago. They were a nuisance to the children's fathers, bay trap-fishermen whose pound nets—long fish traps of stakes and twine set at right angles to the shore—are set in prized locations, the same used by the Indians, who built similar traps of brush and probably gave their blowfish to the children, too.

Through it all, the hard clam meditates in mud or sand, the old reliable of the local fishery since the days when the blue of the clam's shell was coin of the realm, and its dried flesh winter food. The clam, or quahog, is, however, in short supply in the East End's shoaler waters as the population grows and each new family expects its weekend mess o' clams. A mess, on Long Island, is a unit of infinite capacity—that is, enough to feed one's family, however large or small, at a meal.

The clam, like the Indian, probably arrived as the last glacier retreated. Ebb and flow, constant change, yet there has been a natural balance in our world, an equilibrium only yesterday disturbed by a culture that insists on constants in an environment where there can be none, a culture that cannot live with nature but must rule it. Or must have the illusion of rule.

Our bays are still feeding grounds, in the cooler months, for flocks of scoters, despite gunners and oil spills. The scoters feed on small shellfish, as do the chattering black-and-white old squaws and the small flocks of sheldrake. There are broadbill and whistler, too, and sometimes brant. Black duck prefer the ponds and creeks but rest during the day on open water, and in the early summer Canada goslings, from nests on Gardiner's Island, paddle in formation on the bay behind their parents. Once the Labrador duck were here as well, but the last Labrador duck in the world tumbled to a shotgun blast over Gardiner's Bay a century ago. Whose shot? I do not know; an Amagansett relative probably.

In the late 1940s, when the fishermen idled by winter gathered at Promised Land around the big stove in the ramshackle oyster house called City Hall, a skull grinned at the congregation from the top of the kerosene tank. It was all that was left of a walrus, adorned with one and a half tusks, dragged up in a trawl from the bottom way out toward the Hudson Canyon, off to the southward forty or fifty miles where once the Atlantic surf pounded on the beach of a coast pulled out by a receding sea, a sea diminished by the locking up of a portion of the world's water in the great glacier. Was the walrus a chance visitor, carried down from the Arctic aboard an iceberg? Perhaps, for bergs have been seen, even in recent years, as far south as the latitude of Bermuda. I would sooner think he was a fossil, a relic of the last days of the Ice Age, when fierce storms raged along the steep temperature gradient where the edge of cold glacier met warmer sea; when the ice lay two hundred yards thick over Manhattan, on the hills back of Bridgehampton, and over Montauk Point; when frigid streams poured down the silt that would be the South Fork potato fields; when there was no sand bar, no Napeague, no Promised Land.

The walrus was more at ease, no doubt, in that environment than we are in this. The fact that humankind is apparently incapable, in any environment, of perfect contentment is, of course, what distinguishes him from the other animals.

Chapter

XXIV

CERTAINLY INCAPABLE of lasting contentment, and undoubtedly unwilling to admit that man was an animal, was Samuel Buell, East Hampton's pastor from 1746 to 1798. He was described in this century by one of his successors in the East Hampton ministry as a man who "probably exerted more godly influence on the people of his community than any other has done before or since. He stood as a tower of strength in the stormy days of the Revolutionary War, and protected the people against the British soldiery. He directed the founding of Clinton Academy, an influence for good in the community and state." President Ezra Stiles of Yale said of the Reverend Dr. Buell: "This man has done more good than any man who stood on this continent." Another of his contemporaries went somewhat further: "It is probable that very few men, since the days of the Apostles, have been instrumental in the conversion of so many souls as this honored servant of Christ." No matter the number of saved souls; it cannot have been enough for Dr. Buell.

My grandmother called this saintly man an old lecher. She

never saw Samuel Buell, for he had been dead three quarters of a century at her birth, but he was as alive to her as any never-seen but prominent American of her day, and she did not like him any more than she liked, for example, Eugene Debs, some-one else she had not met and did not expect to meet, in this world or the next.

Grandma's acknowledged prejudice was a family matter; I would like to think that mine was more reasoned, developed through seeing in Samuel Buell some of the things that went wrong in the development of this nation's character. The first of my grandmother's family, the Hunttings, to arrive in East Hampton, was the Reverend Nathaniel Huntting, the village's second minister. One of his first social engagements upon coming to Long Island in 1699 from Massachusetts had been that dinner with the pirate Bradish, who had New England "connections" with East Hampton families. Huntting was deposed, after fifty years in his pulpit and at the age of seventy, by James Davenport of the New Lights, who arrived in town and called the old man one of the Jehoshaphats, unconverted and paving the way to hell with his preaching. Buell succeeded Huntting. He was a re-vivalist like Davenport, and while he was not directly responsible for the aged Huntting's retirement, and indeed even persuaded his congregation into a tardy apology for its abandonment of its preacher for a half century, my grandmother shared the Hunttings' resentment. There has always been time on eastern Long Island to cherish old grudges; a population that remains generation after generation on the same ground will remember such things and pass down the reinforcing gossip.

Buell was thirty when he climbed into Huntting's pulpit, a native of Coventry, Connecticut, and a 1741 graduate of Yale. Huntting had received his bachelor's degree from Harvard in 1693 and a master's in 1696. Buell's stepmother was Ulysses S. Grant's great-grandmother, and his first wife, Jerusha Meacham, was kin to Increase and Cotton Mather. Buell had three wives in all; her ancestor Nathaniel, my grandmother pointed out, had married but once. In partial consequence, his family has all but died out today, but then, so have the Buells, sequential marriages or no.

Buell was "converted" at the age of sixteen; that is, although long since baptized, in adolescence he was what some today would call born again. He entered Yale four years later, to find it a battleground of the Great Awakening, a revolt against dogma and reasoned theology. Yale was torn between the leanings of some on the faculty toward Episcopalianism and the inclinations of the New Lights, the party of revival and emotional religious rebirth, toward Presbyterianism. It was a lasting struggle, with roots dating back to the first days of New England, when the bulk of the Puritans were, in essence, nonconforming members of the Church of England, and the Pilgrims were "separated." Nothing ecclesiastical was simple in that day; theology then occupied a people's minds as sports do in the twentieth century, and some of the Puritans were in fact Presbyterians. Their congregations, however, in New England and later on Long Island, were "congregational"—that is, independent—for many years after the settlement, as were their governments in many instances. And the governments were completely intertwined with the local churches.

Although in Southampton on Long Island the "Protistants" of the only permitted church were calling themselves "Presbiterians" as early as 1707, Huntting, a dozen miles away in East Hampton, remained an unconverted "Old Light," and his church was independent, technically "congregational," until the formation of the Long Island Presbytery forty years later. The old preacher was to the end of his days a Latitudinarian, willing to grant leeway in theological belief and practice, with philosophical ties to the old Pilgrim movement. America's colleges were then its seminaries, and if Huntting represented old Harvard, Buell was younger Yale, and Princeton's birth in 1747 as the College of New Jersey was part and parcel of the ferment of the Great Awakening, an event that contributed, if only through rationalist reaction, to the Revolution.

Huntting, for all that he preached an early temperance sermon upon the death of a nine-year-old East Hampton boy from strong drink consumed at a mill raising, was one of the breed of clergy trained in a day when rum was a major article of diet and an ordination an occasion for its consumption in larger-than-usual quantitites. Yet he was a scholar, something his successor, although a man of many talents, was not, and he kept careful records of births and deaths, records which were to be neglected by Buell. It was in Huntting's ministry that the 1717 Church was raised, for many years the largest and grandest on Long Island. Huntting might be taken as representative of an earlier age's more easygoing, worldly clergy; Davenport, who preached against Huntting in East Hampton (Davenport, within his own congregation, distinguished between those whose religion was sound, whom he addressed as "Brethren," and those whose faith was unsound, "Neighbors") was the hard but erratic reformer; and Buell, the smooth follower of the excesses of change.

Yet Buell's reputation had been made in his youth as a traveling revival preacher, licensed by the New Haven Association in the year of his graduation from Yale for service in the Great Revival. He made his way up and down New England, a younger contemporary and pupil of Jonathan Edwards (he preached as his substitute in Northampton, Massachusetts), gaining a reputation as a saver of souls welcome in other pastors' territory because he was "cheerfully subject to the will of the pastors in whose congregations he labored."

He had heard Aaron Burr senior—who had married Jonathan Edwards' daughter, was only a few months older than himself, and was to become president of Princeton and father of one of the great enigma figures of American history—preach with Davenport in East Hampton in 1741. And in 1746 he learned from Burr of Huntting's retirement and sought the vacant post. Jonathan Edwards, old Sinners-in-the-Hands-of-an-Angry-God himself, preached at Buell's installation in East Hampton on September 19, 1746.

Buell found a divided congregation and set about making it

THE BEACH BANKS, BEFORE THE SUMMER HOUSE

whole. Within three years he was able to make his request that those who had earlier separated themselves from the Huntting ministry stand in the church and acknowledge their error. But he did not push the matter. As the Reverend E. E. Eells—pastor of the same flock in the 1930s and a descendant of one of the two unusually named clergymen of the port of Stonington, Connecticut, during the Great Awakening, the Reverends Nathaniel Eells and Joseph Fish—observed, "He did not begin [immediately] to make an effort for a revival in East Hampton, though he was an experienced evangelist." Buell bided his time and led a South Fork version of the Great Revival in 1764. His house in that year, he said, was "filled constantly with sinners and their cries for mercy. Children have come out of Hell's horrors; young people eight, ten, twelve years old have been converted; among the rest a Jew."

In fact, he observed with satisfaction, "the whole town of East Hampton has bowed as one man. Every day the church is filled with worshippers by nine in the morning. Such a praying for mercy is heard; the piercing cries of sinners fill the air. The arrows of conviction have been fastened upon guilty hearts. There are shouts of holy joy and unutterable groanings."

Rev. Buell's constantly filled house, in what is now a small park just west of the East Hampton Free Library, was within earshot of an unutterable groan, within bowshot of an arrow of conviction, of his church, diagonally across grassy Main Street. The Jew was Aaron Isaacs, grandfather of John Howard Payne, the expatriate author of the lugubrious "Home, Sweet Home." Before Buell's death the minister could say, with some small exaggeration and more than a little smug xenophobia, "There is not a separate, a sectarian, or anyone of a different denomination from us in the boundaries of the town."

Aaron Isaacs, even as a Presbyterian, was something new for East Hampton, although there had been Jews in New England and New York for many generations before his East End residency. Indeed, much of what we know about Captain William Kidd's semi-piratical escapades in the Indian Ocean at the end of the seventeenth century comes from a deposition made by one Benjamin Franks, a Jewish jeweler and Danish subject who had failed in business in the West Indies and shipped with Kidd in New York thinking to go to Surrat in India "or any other place where I could best follow my profession." Franks did not like service under Kidd and deserted, returning to New York ahead of the accused pirate. That same spring, as we have seen, Simon Bonan, also a Jew and a jeweler, appears in the East Hampton Town records, once as appraising the gems seized from Colonel Pierson after his embarrassing transaction with Bradish, and again as carrying tax receipts to New York.

Like other towns of Puritan stock, East Hampton, whose faith was largely based upon the Old Testament, seemed to regard the few Jews who passed through as some sort of co-religionists, familiar from Scripture reading if rare in the flesh. This good-natured attitude persisted down through the nineteenth century, until it was overcome by the anti-Semitism accompanying the great waves of immigration in the 1880s.

Wandering Jews were one thing, resident Jews another. It has been said that Aaron Isaacs' headstone in the Old South End Cemetery overlooking East Hampton's Town Pond reads "A Hebrew In Whom There Is No Guile" or a variation on this theme. Perhaps it once did; today, a replacement headstone of fairly recent vintage reads less condescendingly "Aaron Isaacs, 1722–1797."

Isaacs married Mary Hedges. They had eleven children, and my grandmother sometimes pointed out descendants of that union. By her account, they ran to brains and good looks. It went without saying that she attributed these qualities to their Isaacs ancestry, diluted though that might have been. Grandma would have made a good geneticist; she was equally ready to point out, even among relatives, outstanding examples of inbreeding, a natural enough result of the East End's two and a half centuries of isolation.

Eells, in a series of newspaper articles on the history of his church, quoted "President Davis of Hamilton College" on the subject of Buell at East Hampton. Davis' somewhat odd observation was: "Though social and hospitable in his feelings and courteous and affable in his manners, he seldom visited his people, and had but little personal intercourse with them. In his study, however, he always welcomed those who wished for religious instruction; and in cases of sickness, he was ever at hand to administer needed counsel and consolation."

Buell's preaching, for all that it carried a hard doctrine, when read aloud today carries a near-hypnotic bleat, almost musical in effect, full of words sounding well, to be listened to but not necessarily to be comprehended. An example is a sermon delivered in May 1756 to Suffolk companies of Provincial troops setting out for Crown Point and war with the French and Indians. The text is I Chronicles 19:13: "Be of good courage, and let us behave ourselves valiantly for our people, and for the cities of our God: and let the Lord do that which is good in his sight."

> Our war is not undertaken from ambitious views to enlarge our empire or glory, but for our own just and necessary defence, and therefore we may hope for the Lord's assistance in it and that He will crown it with victorious success. And bear in mind ye heroes, that 'tis for the enjoyment and preservation and service of the glorious God, and therefore He will doubtless plead our cause against our enemies. Under these views therefore be courageous and valiant.
>
> Surely the interesting consideration that our cause is just and good, that we are waging in war for the defence of our lives, our liberties, our properties, our Religion; that the Glory of God is concerned herein, and that we may implore His assistance and hope for His blessing, are the most noble motives to banish cowardice and rouse up courage that can ever reign in the breast of officers and soldiers under command.

The chaplain of one of the East End companies marching off for Canada carried a hatchet with which to destroy Papist altars. Dr. Buell remained in East Hampton. The Suffolk regiment included blacks, free and slave; "Molattoes"; "Mustees" (octoroons); and Indians, among them James Warbaton, no doubt kin to Wobetom of the bottle burial. If there were any Catholics among the troops, they doubtless lacked a chaplain.

Chapter **XXV**

THREE DECADES INTO Samuel Buell's ministry in East Hampton, the American Revolution reached Long Island, and Buell was the chief among his townspeople in a time of trouble. The Island was occupied by the British for the entire war after August 1776 and stripped of livestock, fodder and fuel. It was the scene of interminable minor skirmishing, raiding and looting. The traditional view of Dr. Buell's role at this juncture was expressed by Henry P. Hedges in his *History of the Town of East-Hampton*, written in 1897: "The history of that seven years' suffering will never be told. . . . Throughout this period, it is not known that a single Tory lived in the bounds of the town . . . they were true to their country, unterrified, unalterable, devoted Americans. . . . In their difficulties Dr. Buell, their minister, did not abandon them. His talents, ingenuity, wit and mingled prudence and firmness, often averted threatened perils, and rendered important service to his people."

There is a hint here, as in Davis' observation that "he seldom visited his people," of something a bit out of the ordinary. Another Long Island historian, Benjamin F. Thompson, writing in 1839, when there were many alive with personal memories of Buell, was blunter but no less mysterious in the reasons for his judgment: "Buell's life was a checkered scene of good and evil." My grandmother agreed, although she never read the evidence uncovered recently by yet another historian, Dr. Lawrence J. Koncelik, who in 1960 found in the British archives this letter, addressed to William Tryon, Royal Governor of New York Colony:

East Hampton, December 10, 1776

Sir:

Yours by Mr. Hedges came safe to Hand with the Proclamation of Viscount Howes and Williame Howe Esqr. Which publickly read after Divine Worship.—and which I am very sure was very universally assented to, and acquiessed in.—And can assure You, Sir the inhabitents honestly design to remain in a peaceable Obedience to his Majesty, and will not take up Arms, nor encourage others to take up Arms in Opposition to his Authority:—

At the same Time—be equally assured, that should they be compelled to take up Arms against the Continent this east End of the Island is absolutely ruined and Destroyed.—We are so situated that our Condition is insular and extremely critical.— We can't defend ourselves—should the King's troops attempt, we expect they will soon be cut off—

Shipping can't block up the Sound so but that Continental Soldiers Cross.—They and Privateers, at Pleasure—and there are so many of each at, or between us and the Opposite Shore—who visit us often and suddenly—and have already greatly oppressed us— I assure You, Sir, this moment while I am writing I hear of a Number of Continental Soldiers just come into Town.—What number there is at Sagg-Harbour I can't yet find out, nor their design— Judge You, Sir, what our poor Soldiers must do who were designing to set out to morrow morning to wait upon his

Excellency Governor Tryon—some I suppose will not now dare to go—others perhaps will,—tho' they stand a Chance to be transported to the Continent immediately upon their Return.—

I am persuaded, Sir, You pity us in this our unhappy Situation, and You will I doubt not use your Intrest and Influence that we be not necessitated to procure the Resentment of the Continent to our utter Ruin. We have great Confidence in the Benevolence and Clemency of the Kings Officers—hoping that at present we may be suffered to abide in a peaceful Subjection to his Majesty—without becomeing active so as to produce our own Destruction.—

Sir You propose Yours, that I inform Col. Gardiner and other Friends in New-England, concerning the Proclamation You sent me and Benefits to be enjoyed thereby. This I can freely do—and doubt not but the Militia that are gone from us, for fear of being pressed, would with others, gladly return to us, though they stole away, could I assure them, they shall not be pressed into Service—that may cost them their Lives, and in the issue prove the ruin of this End of the Island—

Could Mr. Hand and You, Sir, (our representatives) obtain such a previledge for us?—Happy for us it would indeed be!—As to my own Self, Sir,—I feel myself, a Subject of King George and honestly mean to get in character—I have been so active in getting the Fat Cattle to General Howe—and have so warmly opposed Peoples leaving the Island etc. etc.—that I have been seased and carried down to Sagg-Harbour, in order to be transported to the main—but Indisposition prevented—I now stand upon a People of Honour.—I am however most of all concerned for my Dear People.

We often hear Prophecies from the other Side the Water, that we here shall have an oppressive dreadful Winter—I boldly confront those Prophecies—relying on *British Honour*—and fail not to comfort the fearful—I trust not without sufficient Grounds— If I am mistaken, I shall be confounded and must remain for ever Silent. But tis now after midnight, and I shall weary You, Sir, with reading as well as my Self in writing—

However, I have to add, that I write at the desire of the Principle men in Town—who desire me to inform You—that Dr. Hutcheson is desired and appointed to wait upon his excellency Governor Tryon at this time to represent to his Excellency our peculiarly dangerous and unhappy Situation, as the Gentlemen our Militia Officers can inform You also—

The Dr. has never that I know acted a Part inimical to King or Country—is as well as any man acquainted with our extremely critical situation—which I hope will give the more weight to his Declerations—I was greatly importuned by the Principle Inhabitents in Town to wait upon his Excellency at this Time for the same Purposes—which I had even proposed— But tis not thought safe—the Gentlemen that before urged, withdrew their Petition this evening, since they heard of the coming of Continental Soldiers—as supposing I might thereupon be exposed to immediate Transportation to the Main—

And now, Sir, I am not without Fears, this Letter will be stopped before it goes out of Town— Such are the Times in which we are fallen O You will therefore excuse me, if I subscribe Sir, Yours—etc. etc.

Incognito

Mem. The above wrote by the Revd. Mr. Bewell Presbyterian Minister for the Township of East Hampton—a favorer of the Rebel Rank, untill converted by the Victory of the 27th of August.

The memorandum, with its implicit snigger, was in the hands of Governor Tryon. The Victory of the 27th of August was the Battle of Long Island, a disaster for Washington. Dr. Hutcheson was Dr. Samuel Hutchinson, the village physician, said to be descended from Anne Hutchinson, the contentious New England religious leader of the previous century. Col. Gardiner was

Colonel Abraham Gardiner of East Hampton, a member of the pre-Revolutionary Committee on Correspondence in 1774. His rank was in the militia, and he had forcibly administered the oath of allegiance to the Crown to other East End militia officers less than a month after the Battle of Long Island.

Mr. Bewell, of course, was the Reverend Dr. Samuel Buell, and he was what we would call a collaborationist. Quisling is too strong a word, for he had, after all, been a British subject for most of his life, and indeed had good reason to believe at that writing that he would be one for the rest of it, and concern for his flock was obviously his prime motive in his "Incognito" communication. But he certainly does not qualify as one of Judge Hedges' unterrified, unalterable and devoted Americans of the Revolution.

The war dragged on, and there is little reason to believe that Buell altered his position much during the continuing occupation of Long Island. In the summer of 1780, Admiral Marriot Arbuthnot arrived in Gardiner's Bay with nine ships of the line and a smaller 50-gun ship. He was keeping an eye on the French squadron of the Chevalier de Ternay, which was anchored at Newport, Rhode Island, and wrangling at a distance with his nominal superior, Admiral Sir George Brydges Rodney—newly arrived in New York and flying his flag in the 90-gun ship *Sandwich*—over the chain of command, and more important, prize money.

Arbuthnot took time out from these preoccupations in September of 1780 to invite the gentry of East Hampton to a party aboard the 74-gun *Royal Oak*, his flagship. The locals were led by Colonel Gardiner and the Reverend Dr. Buell, and they dined on curries, including something known as The Devil. Dr. Buell is said to have observed archly that with such spicy food, fruit and women all aboard ship, the consequences might be untoward. Admiral Arbuthnot responded that there were no Eves aboard, a slander on East Hampton's fairest. Dr. Buell sang for his supper with a poem of his own composition:

> On board the *Royal Oak* we are,
> Whose thunders Bourbon's navies fear:
> To Britain's foes she never fails
> to give them laws where e'er she sails.
>
> High in command upon the seas
> She takes or sinks, just as may please
> Her Admiral, great Arbuthnot
> Whose fame shall never be forgot . . .

Dancing ensued. Arbuthnot's squadron, anchored in a long line stretching from Gardiner's Island northwest toward Orient Point, then known as Oyster Ponds, on the North Fork, included the *Culloden* and the *Bedford*, 74s, and the *America*, 64 guns. The following January these three were sent to sea in a blinding northeasterly snowstorm upon news that some of the French vessels were putting out. The *Culloden* struck Shagwong Reef off Montauk, lost her rudder, and fetched up a few hundred yards off Will's Point. This promontory, probably named after Will Indian, a herder mentioned in the East Hampton Town records, was henceforth Culloden Point, and the vessel's bottom and some of her guns rest offshore still.

Most of us have never faced the awful choice before East Hampton during the British occupation, when the Arbuthnot-Rodney quarrel had to be carried on by dispatch boat because the post between New York and East Hampton, even under armed guard, was too dangerous; when hunger was real, and foraging parties of both sides and no sides raided almost nightly; when whaleboat warfare back and forth across Long Island

Sound eventually degenerated into near-piracy; when families were often politically divided. Knowing that a majority of the people of the Thirteen Colonies were probably either British in their sympathies or at best neutral, it is hard to judge Buell. It is easier to find wanting the simplistic history that was ignorant of or ignored the truth of his position during the Revolution, the kind history that has served the nation so poorly. Certainly Buell's fellow townspeople thought little the worse of him after the war, or were perhaps too well aware of the political and moral quandaries that had faced them all to hold his coziness with the British against him. Dr. Buell continued as a community leader and was a moving spirit in the establishment of Clinton Academy, the first school chartered in the State of New York. It opened in 1784, when the guns of the Revolution had barely fallen silent. By then Buell had been a widower, for the second time, for a year. The Academy building, which was probably designed by him, is a handsome monument to his better side, and evidence of his intelligence and architectural skill.

Keeping in mind his unclerical speculation on the possible effect of spices aboard the *Royal Oak*, let us now consider (as did the Reverend Dr. Buell) Mary, daughter of Jeremiah and Ruth Huntting Miller, and great-granddaughter of the Reverend Nathaniel Huntting, who caught the now-aged eye of the cleric. Mary was secretly engaged to a young man, who was unnamed in my grandmother's reminiscences of a tale told to her in her childhood. The youth, she said, was of good family and character but an unbeliever; the Millers would not have him. But Buell, they would.

Dr. Ebenezer Sage, who had set up in rival practice to Dr. Hutchinson in East Hampton after his graduation from Yale in 1778, commented upon the event in a letter to a friend in November 1785:

This day was married the Rev. Samuel Buel aged 71, to Miss Mary Miller aged 17; upward of half a century's difference—Alas! poor depraved humanity. This old man with one foot in the grave—his body withered to a mummy—his face shrivelled like a baked apple—on his head a few solitary hairs—his nose like a shoemaker's awl—his eyes sunk into their sockets—his teeth worn out by mastication, and torn away by the hand of time with here and there a lonely stump—deaf, and almost blind—his bones merely rattling in their skin like beans in a bladder—his brain so far wasted that punning and storytelling make up the greater part of his conversation—and, for all this, he must have a young girl to toy and trifle with. What a lesson this is to teach the frailty of our natures—the imbecility and vanity of old age, and period of dotage and second childhood. Alas! poor old man. Surely, as the saying is, they must be fools together.

Buell was perhaps in his second childhood, although Sage stretched matters by adding two years to the bridegroom's age and subtracting two from the bride's, but he was still preaching. Some Sundays after the wedding, according to Grandmother, the minister took as his text David's lust for Bathsheba, wife of Uriah. Buell described how Nathan the prophet told David the story of the rich man, with exceeding many flocks and herds, who took the poor man's one little ewe lamb, and then, as David, Buell announced to his congregation: "As the Lord liveth, the man that hath done this thing shall surely die."

From the back pew Mary Miller's former affianced rose up, pointed at the minister, and roared out Nathan's answer: "Thou art the man!" Buell lived for another fourteen years and indeed sired one last child, another Jerusha, a name borne by his first wife and two dead infants in between. He lives on in local memory as a great patriot and spiritual leader.

Is it possible, let alone fair, to judge such a man at such a distance, or to see in him writ small some flaws which have loomed larger in the American character? Several portraits of Buell show him as possessing a harsh mouth, a firm jaw, a nose like an ax, and eyes cast somewhat down and squinting. A portrait of Huntting as a much younger man shows him with a round face, full lips, and large dark eyes, the same look my great-uncle Dan Huntting has in photographs taken at an equivalent age. Nathaniel Huntting in portrait looks somewhat Mediterranean; Buell all New England.

From his portraits Buell, whose doctorate was bestowed by Dartmouth in his old age, appears to have been a small man. His world was small, too. His charge, East Hampton, was proportionately far greater in that world, particularly in the American colonies, than it is today. Suffolk County had perhaps 10,000 inhabitants when Buell assumed the ministry at East Hampton, which contained about 1,000 of those souls. New York City was an overgrown village with a population of around 15,000.

In the religious sense, Protestant North America was an extended village, and eastern Long Island was an important neighborhood in it. Hence the interest of such figures as Burr, Stiles, and Edwards. It was a small world but a hard one, far less understood by its inhabitants than is ours, and Buell's congregations literally prayed for an understanding of it and its frequent horrors. The minister's long life began in the reign of George I, and he lived to know, and no doubt abhor, the Directory in France, and an Infidel Society in East Hampton. The New Light of 1741 was old doctrine indeed by the end of Buell's days in 1798, yet the public demand for dynamic churchly oratory never flagged. Buell's successor was another Yale graduate, Lyman Beecher, who rode to national fame on his sermon preached at East Hampton and elsewhere upon the death of Hamilton at the hand of Aaron Burr junior:

When we intrust life, and liberty, and property to the hands of men, we desire some pledge of their fidelity. But what pledge can the duelist give? His religious principle is nothing . . . his moral principle is nothing. . . . The honor of a dueling legislator does not restrain him in the least from innumerable crimes which affect the peace of society. . . . He may be a gambler, prodigal, a fornicator, an adulterer, a drunkard, a murderer, and not violate the laws of honor. . . .

We are murderers, a nation of murderers, while we tolerate and reward the perpetrators of the crime. . . .

This angry man is remembered today as the father of an equally angry daughter, the Abolitionist Harriet Beecher Stowe, and of the amorous Henry Ward Beecher, who shared with Buell some attributes of saint and Satan.

Chapter
XXVI

DR. BUELL PREACHED on David's lust in the 1717 Church from the pulpit occupied before him by Nathaniel Huntting, for the latter two thirds of that cleric's long pastorate, and after him by Lyman Beecher. The church, which was hung with a bell given by Queen Anne, was torn down in 1871 after East Hampton's Presbyterians decided they needed a new edifice more in keeping with the times. They built a larger church, and it was termed schooner-rigged by local sailormen; its easterly steeple, which came to a point, was seen as the foremast, somewhat shorter, in true schooner fashion, than the mainmast, a flat-topped steeple ringed with a wrought-iron fence. We climbed up there as youngsters, when we could find the key hidden by the clock winder and bell puller, to sneak cigarettes and meet girls; the view out over the elms to the sea was magnificent. Since then the Presbyterians have turned the building into more of a New England church, with a single pointed spire and no loafing place.

When the 1717 Church was torn down, its timbers and planks, said to have been Gardiner's Island lumber, were bought by Lew

Jones, a master carpenter who built a house from them on upper Newtown Lane, just north of the spot where the railroad tracks would cross the lane two decades later. Carpenter Jones built slowly and well; he is said to have planed the undersides of floor timbers which would be visible only to those who, as he did with his plane, slid on their backs under a cellarless portion of the house. His less amiable eccentricities included catching rats and roasting them alive in a wire trap of the old eel-pot type and sawing off the bill of a woodpecker, which he then released. It flew away, he said, croaking "Maturity, maturity." His house still stands.

The 1717 Church faced Dr. Buell's Clinton Academy across Main Street. The academy, now a museum, houses the pulpit of the church, its weather vane, the face of its clock, a fine contemporary portrait of Dr. Buell in a wig, and the very wig itself. I was rummaging one day up in the highest loft of our family barn, above the unheated, uninsulated room occupied at the turn of the century by Spencer Quaw, my grandfather's part black, part Indian stable hand, farm hand, and part-time fisherman. The barn stands two or three hundred yards from the site of the old church, and less than that distance in another direction from the site of Samuel Buell's home. Rearranging the accumulated junk of several centuries, I found a little white door about three and a half feet tall and twenty inches wide, with a small panel above a larger, marked with a rusty iron plate below a molded rail that showed traces of a yellowish stain and old varnish. It looked familiar; it was a mate to a pew door from the 1717 Church in the Clinton Academy museum. One of the Hedges family, who then owned the barn, probably salvaged it when the church was torn down in 1871; perhaps it was the door of the Hedges pew.

The church was followed on the site by McCann's Meat Market, a flimsy two-story Victorian building since removed to the summer colony and transformed into an elegant home. In my boyhood the Meat Market shared the end of East Hampton's Main Street that now bears a faint resemblance to Colonial Williamsburg with the drugstore building, which now houses the weekly newspaper, the *Star,* Otto Simmons' plumbing-supply shop, and in the Simmons building, a liquor store. Mr. Simmons also sold gasoline, and from time to time other boys and I would be left to tend the single hand-cranked gas pump while he was off, by my recollection, playing golf, unlikely pastime as that was for a plumber of his generation. During his absences we searched the toilet which he kept in the show window to spite the Ladies Village Improvement Society. We did not touch the pint of whiskey customarily hidden in its dry tank, but we always examined the pack of playing cards kept there for Dr. Simmons' poker-playing, whiskey-sipping cronies. The cards, we decided, were French; they were illustrated with photographs that were an adequate substitute for the sex-education classes the East Hampton schools lacked. The old men could not play cards when we were present (they did not know we were well aware of the pack), so they told stories. From them I learned such useful information as how to make the best July Fourth explosion of them all—it involves a pound of black powder, lots of newspaper, a quart or two of axle grease, and an anvil—and how Harrison Mulford lost the bet when he claimed he could identify any wood by the taste. They tricked him with a punky bit of the backboard of his own privy.

Those years were, of course, the years before zoning became fashionable, when, even in East Hampton, liquor stores and meat markets and libraries could exist doorstep-to-doorstep, when rural America was a place of wrecked cars rusting in unmown dooryards, when a man could put a sign or a billboard on his own property whenever or however he pleased. Burma Shave still ruled the highways, barns were for painted slogans, and free enterprise was more or less just that.

Free enterprise, yes, if you were free, white, and twenty-one, a catch phrase that has gone the way of the Burma Shave signs. There was a powwow one September back in those days at our old picnic place at Springy Banks on the west side of Three Mile Harbor, north of East Hampton. Most of the Indians on hand were from the West, whole carloads of redskins in old Buicks, Oldsmobiles, and Cadillacs bearing plates from states like Oklahoma and Wyoming, states where they would not be able to vote or drink for another few decades. We watched as one lank old buck, visible penis wrapped mummy-style beneath his loose loincloth, danced alone.

Yi! Yi! Yi! Yi! he chanted, bare feet pounding against the packed sand, and feathers bouncing. *Ooogha! Ooogha! Ooogha! Ooogha!* responded a middle-aged black man, whom we then called a Negro, from high up in a nearby tree, pounding his chest in imitation of the gorilla in a Tarzan movie. He swung from a branch by one hand while scratching his armpit with the other, and his family watched in horror.

I knew him and knew that he, like a good many other members of "old" black families on the East End of Long Island, was probably as Indian as some of the dancers, as Indian as poor Spenny Quaw, on whom, my grandmother told me approvingly, the Irish servant girl had once turned the garden hose when he "got fresh." The man in the tree, and his family, had chosen Negritude. They could have picked Indianhood, but never, in a nation which at that time and in some parts still considered an eighth part "Negro blood" as grounds for legal segregation, could they have joined the white majority.

Springy Banks, where the Indians danced, is part of the Hampton Waters subdivision now, and the hollow tree trunks sunk in the springs at the foot of the bluff, supposedly by the Indians, as wells, have long since rotted away. I once tried to tell a woman who lived in a new house, built just where the Indians had danced, about the powwows, and the unmarked graves on the hill behind, and our childhood picnics on what we had naïvely assumed to be public land. My grandmother had camped there with her female friends in the early 1900s, I said; a group of women in their late twenties with children already entering their teens, smoking cigarettes and digging clams and singing around fires in an attempt to regain the girlhoods abruptly ended when they had married a decade or so earlier at sixteen and seventeen. The woman of the new house grew very angry and said we resented outsiders like her. I hadn't meant it that way.

There are no more powwows at Springy Banks, but the tourists still flock each Labor Day weekend to the Shinnecock Indian Pow-Wow in Southampton, a benefit for the Reservation Church. Some of them titter when they realize that a good many of the Shinnecocks are of mixed black-white-red ancestry, in proportions as varied and pleasing, to the unbigoted, as in the population of some West Indian islands.

That this should be so is not strange. Blacks came to Long Island very early, quite possibly with the first Dutch settlers at the West End and with the English to the East End some years later. There were free blacks on the Island in Colonial times, but most of them must have come as slaves and been thrown together in labor at the bottom of the social heap with Indians, freed slave and indentured, and indentured whites. All slavery in New York State ended in 1827, with provision for life-long tenancy where desired, but the indenture system lasted much longer. Casper Bedell, East Hampton Village's police chief in my boyhood, had come to East Hampton at the turn of the century as a "bound-boy," an indentured youngster from a poor or broken family, or from an orphanage. There may still be old men living who were bound-boys.

Slavery, of course, was a far cry from indenture, cruel though that system may have been at times. No one knows when the first slaves came to the South Fork, although it seems certain that among the black families here today are descendants of First Families with as valid a claim upon the title as the whitest of whites, and certain blacks and whites with an aboriginal heritage who have a right to laugh along with the Indians at the very idea of First Families. As early as 1687, there were 26 slaves in East Hampton Town, and 35 indentured servants, out of a population of 563, not counting Indians, who perhaps numbered several hundred. In 1698 Southampton had 83 blacks and 152 Indians in a population of somewhat over 600. Suffolk was inhabited by 2,679 people in that year, 2,121 of them white.

A year later, when Captain Kidd visited Gardiner's Island, he asked John Gardiner "to carry three Negroes, two boys and a girl, ashore to keep till he the said Kidd or his Order should call for them . . . about two hours after the Narrator had got the said Negroes ashore, Captain Kidd sent his boat ashore with two bailes of Goods and a Negro Boy." Kidd had just returned from the Indian Ocean; one would like to know the story of these four unfortunates, natives probably of East Africa or Madagascar, landed on a foreign shore like so much merchandise. Were they taken, like his bailes of Goods, from some ship of the Mogul Augangzeb? Won at cards from the pirates at Johanna? Captured in some tribal war and bought from a victorious chieftain? Or simply kidnapped somewhere north of the Cape of Good Hope?

Nathaniel Huntting kept a careful list of deaths during his pastorate at East Hampton, from the last years of the seventeenth century through the first half of the eighteenth, but "only of English & not negro or Indian, slaves or servants." His successor,

Samuel Buell, listed deaths "of baptized only." This, however, included Christian blacks, if not Indians, whose conversion had become a Presbyterian concern at the time of the Great Awakening and the beginning of Buell's pastorate, but who were still regarded somewhat as Roger Williams had described them a century earlier: "Wolves endewed with mens braines."

DOWN HOOK, EAST HAMPTON, 1900

There had been free blacks in East Hampton at least as early as 1676, when "John Neiger" was granted permission to build a house in the public highway near "Mrs. Codners"—that is, near James Lane and the village seat of the Gardiners of Gardiner's Island. The house was to revert to the Town upon his death or moving away. More than a century and a half later, however, men could still be chattels, and this was the point of the South

Fork's sole nationally significant entry in the long ledger of black-white relations in the United States.

On August 26, 1839, the Revenue brig *Washington* came upon a schooner anchored at Fort Pond Bay, Montauk, off the point where H.M.S. *Culloden* had driven ashore fifty-eight years earlier. The schooner was the *Amistad*, under the command of Cinque, a slave who had led a successful mutiny against the slaveship's captain and crew. Cinque and his men were headed, they thought, back to Africa. The *Washington*, according to one of her officers, found "a number of people on the beach with carts and horses, and a boat passing to and fro . . . The negroes were found in communication with the shore, where they laid in a fresh supply of water, and were on the point of sailing again for the coast of Africa. They had a good supply of money, some of which it is likely was taken by the people on the beach. After disarming and sending them on board from the beach, the leader jumped overboard with three hundred doubloons about him, the property of the captain, all of which he succeeded in losing from his person, and then submitted himself to be captured."

Among the men ashore were two from Sag Harbor, Captain Henry Green and Pelatiah "Duke" Fordham, a prominent tavern keeper and a friend of James Fenimore Cooper, who lived there for some time. Green and Fordham later disputed with the Revenue Service a claim to Cinque and his fifty-four fellow Africans; the suspicion that they had somehow obtained some of the cash aboard the *Amistad* was apparently current in the Sag Harbor of their day. The issue of the ownership of Cinque and his men went to the Supreme Court and played a major part in the growth of the Abolition movement, in which the Beechers, long since removed from East Hampton, were by that time involved.

That confrontation at Fort Pond Bay is a scene Bertolt Brecht might have written: the *Amistad* at anchor, tattered sails left set, for the blacks knew little of seamanship; the approach of the Revenue brig, whose crew saw Cinque and his companions as property, as prize money; more whites ashore, equally greedy, conniving on the rocky beach. The effect is heightened by our later knowledge that Cinque, returned to Africa as a free man by a landmark decision of the United States Supreme Court, spent his declining years as a trader in slaves.

"THOSE WAS THE HAPPY DAYS," Maria Fowler Pharaoh Banks recalled in 1936, when she was eighty-eight, and thinking of her youth on Montauk, before she and the others of her tribe were dispossessed. "Those was the happy days and how I have longed to be back home and live the same life over again, but it is too late now. Those days will never return."

It happened so:

Well, there was a man come to see me a year before I moved off and offered me so much money and told me such sweet lies. I found out after. How he would give me $80 a year and he would see that I would never be sorry, for he would educate my children. He did not. The $80 a year he told me he would give me as long as I lived, it was to be always, I got it a few years and no more. This gentleman's name was Frank S. Benson [son of Arthur, the 1879 purchaser of Montauk]. My children was to have this money. Also, there is one girl left, Pocahontas, and if she was treated right and got what she was supposed to have she would not have to work so as she does for her living. It makes me feel very sorry for her.

Pocahontas may have been a girl to her eighty-eight-year-old mother, but she was well along in years herself in 1936 and worked for her living as a charwoman in the East Hampton switchboard room of the New York Telephone Company until shortly before her death in 1963 at the age of eighty-four. I remember her sitting in a car by the curb in front of the Telephone office during a strike in the late 1950s. There were pickets, something unusual in East Hampton, and Pocahontas looked puzzled, uncertain as to whether she should cross the picket line. She was a familiar figure at parades and fairs, a stocky woman in a buckskin dress, sometimes making her oak kitchen scrubs in Montauk style, round-handled.

Maria Fowler Pharaoh Banks's bitter memories continued:

> After my husband died I came off to East Hampton to live in the winter with my sister Olive Butler, and someone set my house on fire and burned it flat to the ground. Someone also burned my father's house down. They stole everything we had in the houses, for we went to Montauk after we moved off and found the house had been broken in and most everything was gone and all my husband's papers, anything that was any good.

Wyandank Pharaoh saw the issue in broader terms in a 1916 letter to the East Hampton *Star*:

> Why does the paper talk that there is no Montauk Indians? As far as this being a queer world it is true in this world. It really does seem too bad to think the whites should go on their lands to take their livelihood away from them, we should say that it was a queer world. Plenty of law but very little justice. This surely seems as though this was a rich man's world. The

decision that Justice Abel S. Blackmore gave in the court and that there was not enough Montauk Indians to go back to live the tribal rights. There was nothing said that there wasn't any Montauk Indians. He knew better. . . .

From eastern Long Island to the Pacific, the North American Indians—who are acknowledged to have had little comprehension of, and when they did comprehend, little sympathy for, European notions of land tenure—have demonstrated again and again their own identity with the land. The Montauks, in the late nineteenth and early twentieth centuries, kept coming back to Indian Field on the Montauk peninsula, exercising privileges guaranteed to them by their 1660 sale to the Proprietors of Montauk, which they believed remained in force with the Proprietors' successor in title, Arthur Benson. They did so in the face of repeated court decisions against them, threats, and the fact of accepted quit-claim payments by some of their fellows. It was all they had left, of course; from the earliest days of the English settlement, restrictions on the Indians' seasonal migrations were imposed, limits and boundaries were established, and the Indians were gradually pushed into small corners of their former holdings, such as the Shinnecock Reservation at Southampton, a tract now immensely valuable, ironically enough.

There is talk today of a Shinnecock suit which might regain for the tribe adjoining properties, including the Southampton and National golf links, a prospect that would have brought instant apoplexy to the muttonchopped late-nineteenth-century founders of these havens of the reclusive rich. Those founders employed young Shinnecocks as their first caddies and were set back on their heels when some of the caddies rapidly became better golfers than their employers. On second thought . . .

A sentimentalist view of Indian territoriality is severely shaken by such a convincing work of revisionist history as Lynn Ceci's

"Effect of European Contact and Trade on the Settlement Pattern," the doctoral dissertation on the wampum industry referred to earlier and published by University Microfilms International. Dr. Ceci argues that before European contact, Long Island was occupied only seasonally by mainland aborigines in small numbers, and that year-round occupation and indeed the web of political alliances dominated by such figures as Wyandanch (who may have been poisoned by fellow Indians not as inclined as he toward cooperation with the whites) were the result of economic pressures—that is, the Dutch-British struggle over furs and wampum. Long Island was no doubt the great wampum manufactory, its aboriginal inhabitants in effect wage-slaves therein, small gears in the great English trade system.

And where does that leave the Indians and their descendants, and their claims, literal and figurative, on Long Island, on North America itself? If there were only a few hundred Montauks at the time of the European settlement, and if their name itself was half-breed—the French *meteaux* for the steel drill used in wampum making combined with the Algonquin suffix *hock*, meaning "men of"—what difference does it make?

If the Meteauhock-Montauks wandered, if they had no sense of land titles, if they would "sell" their land half a dozen times over, does that change the fact that they were of the land, part of an essentially unchanging ecological balance, for possibly 120 centuries before they were set to work making wampum for Englishmen to trade to other Indians, equally innocent of advanced theories of property, for furs to keep the wealthy of Europe warm? This land was theirs; today it is not. Perhaps, like improvident tenants, they deserved eviction, but if they did, the premises remain haunted by their long occupation.

Forget the derivations: Montauk-meteaux . . . Massapequa, Dutch for marsh-trading-place, disillusionments which, once absorbed, will blur clear old romantic notions about the Indian into the smeared, complicated page that is always closer to historical reality. Forget analytics, and remember that the Indians were storytellers, fantasizers, people of the Word as the English were people of the Book.

And the words that they left are many: raccoon, opossum, old squaw, moccasin, samp (the hulled-corn porridge of Long Island winters still), caucus (yes), papoose, seapoose (the run-out tide-rip that drowns its quota of ocean bathers each summer), pung, the work-sled, wigwam, quahog, squash, totem, toboggan, wood-chuck (again, yes), the scuppernong grape, hickory, pone, tamarack, succotash, tomahawk, and, finally, wampum, possibly the local root of evil, as Tammany (a chief of the Delawares) may be of Manhattan.

Then there are the place-names: Georgica, Napeague, Accabonac, Wamponamon, Wickapogue, Pantigo, Sagaponack, Amagansett, Apaquogue, Shagwong, Mecox, Agawam—rolling, full approximations of sounds none of us have ever heard, more or less accurate echoes of words and combinations of words whose meanings scholars argue. These are Long Island names; every corner of the nation has its quota of these remembrances, tangled transliterations from a dozen languages and a hundred dialects.

Consider, too, the Indian as individual, remembering that the names as set down in the records were by-ear renderings by scribes who were far from sure in their transcription of common English names, even their own, which they sometimes spelled differently from day to day; that the Europeans jovially clapped names from ancient history, particularly pagan history, upon red as well as black; and that women, even English women, were rarely a party to the sort of dry business reported in seventeenth-century Town records:

Chigonoo, hired for "burneing Meahtauk," 1682; Papasequin, a Muntaucut, 1685 (Papa-Sequin, a small French coin); his son,

Quausuk; the whalers of 1681—Ungomunt, Jambasun, Sasak-
takon, Unquonomon, Muddoah, Plato Indian, Will Indian; the
whalers of 1682—Menan, Hary, Shine, Samson; another whaler,
a year later, Hector, alias Akeatum; a gin-keeper or cattle-tender
in 1683, "The Indian Called Quagohi & by the English Harry";
Obadia the engiane; Issaack; Mech Graes, which we would spell
Much Grease.

John Mahue. Natt "allias Jyampais." Ben Indian. Jephery.
Jephreys Squaw. Abel "alies Tomhage." Quasequeg "and his
squa." Onadiah. Chikano. Paneso. Vugowont. Awampequid.
Hannibal. Magoe. Ned. Sedumps. Wichaboage. Suckanokou.
Gentleman. Shotnose. Livewell. Addam. Wewete Sowet.
Pemeson. Weomp. Hoboneck. Hames. Weaumpe. Reassowunk.
Jambasha. Scanderbeg. Wombanocum. Japhet. Dick. Mutta-
baune. Pauwasik. Tachumme. Aswubashneag. "An indian Cap-
tive girle about Thirteene or foorteen years of age commonlie
called or known by ye name of Beck." The date, 1678, her sale
to James Loper of East Hampton, and its place, New London,
indicates that she was a survivor of the massacre called by the
English the Great Swamp Fight, at Kingston, Rhode Island, in
December 1675.

The Poosepatucks, Montauks, Shinnecocks, and Matinecocks
of Long Island are today reputed to sense when another of their
dwindling number has died, and they arrive uninvited at the
funeral.

If these quiet brown- and black-skinned people, carpenters
and fishermen and factory workers, are descendants of Roger
Williams' "wolves endewed with men's braines," so are we all.
If Bernal Díaz, passing through Zocotlán on the way to the
conquest of the City of Mexico with Cortés counted more than a
hundred thousand sacrificed skulls piled neatly in a plaza, the
Conquistadors fresh from the land of the Inquisition were quite
as adept at torture as were the Indians—and as were the other

European settlers of North America, trained as they were on a continent torn by religious wars of the utmost ferocity.

In 1649, within a year of East Hampton's settlement, the English cousins and brothers of the local founding fathers chopped off the head of their King. Eleven years later, at the Restoration, ten of the Regicide judges were suspended by their necks, eviscerated, quartered, and finally beheaded, with heads and hearts displayed to the populace. This was drawing and quartering, and it may have been more merciful than the pressing to death of New England witches later in that century, or the electrical roasting accorded indigent rapists and hyphenated-American spies by United States justice in this century.

Woodrow Wilson, like his predecessor as president of Princeton, Aaron Burr senior, a repository of the Puritan tradition, once called the United States the only idealistic nation in the world. Perhaps. But as Aaron Burr junior was the grandson of old Jonathan Edwards himself, our national inheritance has its somber aspects, and we can no more escape them than could the young and cynical Burr.

Long Island's inheritance, accumulated over four and a half centuries of European presence and the previous millennia of aboriginal occupation, is a microcosm of the continent's. What happened in this little northeasterly corner of the continent is more or less what happened everywhere else, although not always in the same order or in synchronization with greater happenings. On eastern Long Island, probably because of the tardy arrival of the railroad—trains reached East Hampton almost three decades after they had spanned the nation—the long middle spell of North America's development from a hunting to an industrial economy was protracted to a degree that drew wide attention. Writers for *Harper's* and other influential magazines of the late nineteenth and early twentieth centuries on several occasions wrote with some wonder about the quaint Hamptons, holdout bastions of the Colonial verities. They ignored such embarrassments as congenital syphilis, endemic in a few East End families until the advent of penicillin in my late childhood.

The East End was, in *Harper's* heyday, a backwater. But it had not always been so. In Colonial days, when the Europeans occupied a thin belt along the Atlantic, Southampton and East Hampton, with populations of around a thousand souls each, were proportionately far larger in the general population. Situated on the border of New England and the Middle Atlantic colonies, at the meeting place of Dutch and English influence, theological battlegrounds between various strains of Puritanism and with theocratic town governments locked in dogged Low Church battle with the High Church Colonial government of New York for many decades, the East End Towns included many more than the usual number of strands of seventeenth- and eighteenth-century North American society, strands which were to come together into the rope of the United States.

A backwater yes, but a backwater that regularly floated passengers on the great tides of America. Within half a century of its settlement—a settlement itself carried out by younger sons and the already land-poor of Massachusetts—the South Fork had in its turn sent out settlers to New Jersey. It had dispatched a whaler, James Loper (with his slave Beck?), to Nantucket, to teach the art of whaling. It had received, in the year 1699—the year when the Indian Ocean piracy erupted to send Kidd and dozens more back to the Eastern Seaboard of North America—its dark strangers, bolts of cloth of gold, and bags of silver. Eastern Long Island's trade with the West Indies was by then well under way, and before another century was out, its deep-sea whaling was well established, and its privateers had crossed and recrossed the Atlantic. The whaling would continue for another hundred years and take East End seamen to all the world's oceans.

On land, every East End family had its representatives in the march westward, through New York State, Ohio, Indiana, Illinois, Kansas, and finally California. The Montauks, too, went west, many of them; there are remnants of the tribe in Wisconsin, at Brotherton, a hopefully named Indian settlement of the early 1800s. Sag Harbor's Argonauts went to the Gold Rush, a shipload of quibbling captains. Some of their sons hunted buffalo in western Kansas a generation later, and the next generation sent sons and perhaps daughters to the Yukon, where a Montauk Bluff hangs over the river for which the territory was named. Some of them went to the Philippines, Cuba, and China. Now the frontier is closed.

At home, as it went in North America so it went in the old East Riding of Long Island. Clearing of the land for agriculture went hand in hand with hunting, and the payment of bounties takes up a good deal of space in the Town records for the first century of the settlement. On the water, the hunting of whales was a major source of income for two and a half centuries, and fishing and shellfishing remain bulwarks of the East End economy. Farming, too, is still important, but except to those few who make their living directly from it, it is only as a pleasant adjunct to a larger resort economy.

Eastern Long Island's society was agrarian long after the United States became a major industrial nation. Going west on Long Island remains in a way a trip forward in time. The line between rural-resort and outer suburbia is as clear as the line of smog visible on a sunny day somewhere up toward Patchogue, some fifty miles east of Manhattan, which is about where the small temples of that late-twentieth-century chimera of the tax-conscious outer-suburban, light industry, first appeared. Farther west, in Nassau County, the clock reverses itself, and one is traveling backward toward the brick warehouses and tall chimneys of the late nineteenth century until, through the

Industrial Revolution stench of the rendering plants in Long Island City, one sights the twin towers of Babel and the declining years of the twentieth century, the World Trade Center, looming over lower Manhattan.

Digging for the Center's foundations, workmen found timbers of a ship buried deep in the muck of what was once the east bank of the Hudson. Some think they were part of Adriaen Block's *Tyger*, burned there before he explored Long Island Sound to Block Island in 1614.

$\mathcal{S}$ources

No truly comprehensive modern history of Long Island exists, and its geology has been likewise neglected. Local histories abound, printed folklore flourishes, and most geology texts contain either some reference to Long Island's features or explain them in the general sense. Long Island reference material is thus plentiful, but thin on the ground. In this work, the several hundred books and pamphlets on Long Island contained in the East Hampton *Star*'s reference library were a primary source. More important, however, were the extensive files of my late mother, Jeannette Edwards Rattray, and the spiral notebooks filled by her mother, Florence Huntting Edwards, bless her. Grandma did not trust us to remember and pass on orally, as she had, the grandmother's tales of three centuries. She was right, as usual. The major references used in this book were:

Adams, James Truslow. *History of the Town of Southampton (East of Canoe Place)*. (Hampton Press, 1918).

———. *Memorials of Old Bridgehampton* (Hampton Press, 1916). Early work by a great American historian.

Black, Robert C. III. *The Younger John Winthrop* (Columbia University Press, 1966). The New England–Long Island Connection.

Bonomi, Patricia U. *A Factious People: Politics and Society in Colonial New York* (Columbia University Press, 1971).

Ceci, Lynn. *The Effect of European Contact and Trade on the Settlement Pattern of Indians in Coastal New York, 1524–1665: The Archaeological and Documentary Evidence* (Xerox University Microfilms, Ann Arbor, Mich., 1977). The Great Wampum Conspiracy.

East Hampton Town Records 1648–1943. Deciphered and privately printed in nine volumes between the years 1887 and 1957. Full sets are hard to find, the tome for the exciting years 1701–1734 being in short supply.

East Hampton Town Trustees Records, 1725–1955. Printed by the Town at odd intervals over the years 1926–1957; a sorry chronicle of the long erosion of a public trust.

Edwards, Everett J., and Rattray, Jeannette Edwards. *Whale Off! The Chronicle of American Shore Whaling* (Stokes, 1933).

Engineers, United States Army Corps of. *Cooperative Beach Erosion Control and Interim Hurricane Study, Fire Island Inlet to Montauk Point, 1958.* The Beach Bible, like the other Good Book a continuing source of argument but packed with information.

Epstein, Jason, and Barlow, Elizabeth. *East Hampton: A History and Guide* (Medway Press, 1975). Current and accurate.

Filer, Hugh C. *Life in East Hampton Seventy Years Ago* (privately printed, 1967). East Hampton Confidential.

Gardiner, David. *Chronicles of East Hampton* (privately printed, 1871). Gentlemanly essays, recently reprinted.

Gardiner, John Lion. *Gardiners of Gardiners Island* (Star Press, 1927). All of 'em, 585 in the male line as of that year, individually numbered like prize steaks.

Jameson, John Franklin. *Privateering and Piracy in the Colonial Period: Illustrative Documents* (Macmillan, 1923). Treasure!

Morison, Samuel Eliot. *The European Discovery of America, the Northern Voyages, A.D. 500–1600* (Oxford University Press, 1971).

Murphy, Robert Cushman. *Fish-Shape Paumanok: Nature and Man on Long Island* (American Philosophical Society, 1964). Slim, but one of the best books on the subject.

Muster Rolls, New York Provincial Troops, 1755–1764 (New York Historical Society, 1892). A lot livelier than it sounds.

Osborn, Oliver. Unpublished diary, 1870s. Lent by the late Amy Osborn Bassford.

Prime, Nathaniel S. *History of Long Island, N.Y.* (Robert Carter, 1845).

Rattray, Jeannette Edwards. *East Hampton History and Genealogies* (Country Life Press, 1953).

———. *Ship Ashore! A Record of Maritime Disasters of Montauk and Eastern Long Island, 1640–1955* (Coward-McCann, 1955).

———. *Up and Down Main Street* (East Hampton Star, 1968). Old East Hampton houses and people.

Rodney, Admiral Lord. *Letter-Books and Order-Book.* 2 vols. (New York Historical Society, 1932).

Schmitt, Frederick P., and Schmid, Donald E. *H.M.S. Culloden* (Mystic, Conn.: Marine Historical Association, 1961).

Sleight, Harry D. *Sag Harbor in Earlier Days* (Hampton Press, 1930). Cantankerous, idiosyncratic, and marvelous.

Sterling, Dorothy. *The Outer Lands, A Natural History Guide to Cape Cod, Martha's Vineyard, Nantucket, Block Island, and Long Island* (Norton, 1967).

Thompson, Benjamin F. *History of Long Island* (E. French, 1839). A basic work and fairly easy to find.

Most of these books are contained in the Long Island Collection at the East Hampton Free Library, an excellent place for research. The Robert Keene Bookshop in Southampton can usually find individual titles. Some are now available in softcover reprint, sometimes in facsimile reproduction.

Index